Harvey Benge

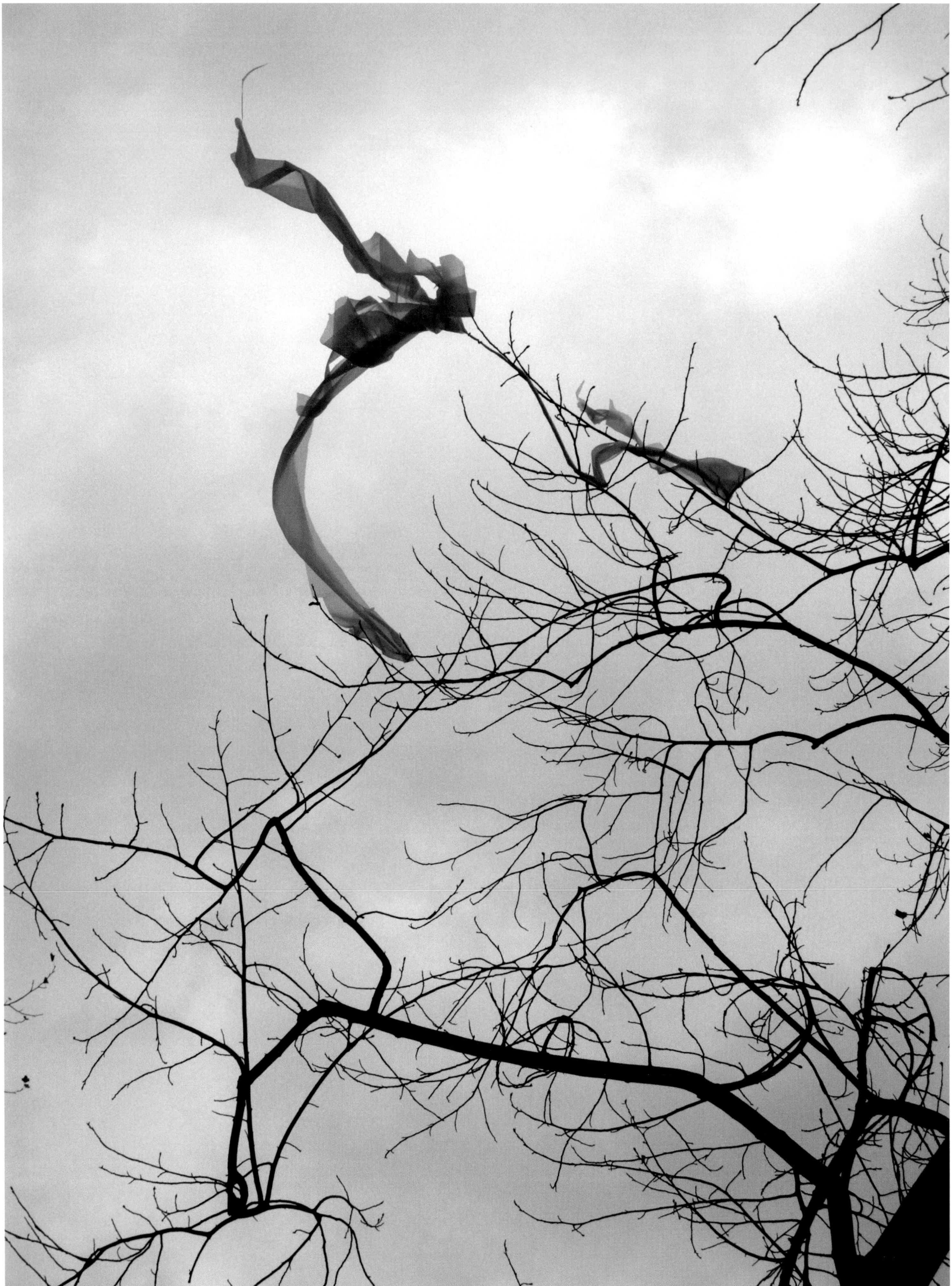

ALL THE PLACES I'VE EVER KNOWN

Harvey Benge

KEHRƎR

Since everything is but an apparition \\ Perfect in being what it is \\

Having nothing to do with good or bad \\ Acceptance or rejection \\ You might as well burst out laughing!

Longchenpa (Longchen Rabjampa, 1308 – 1364)

01

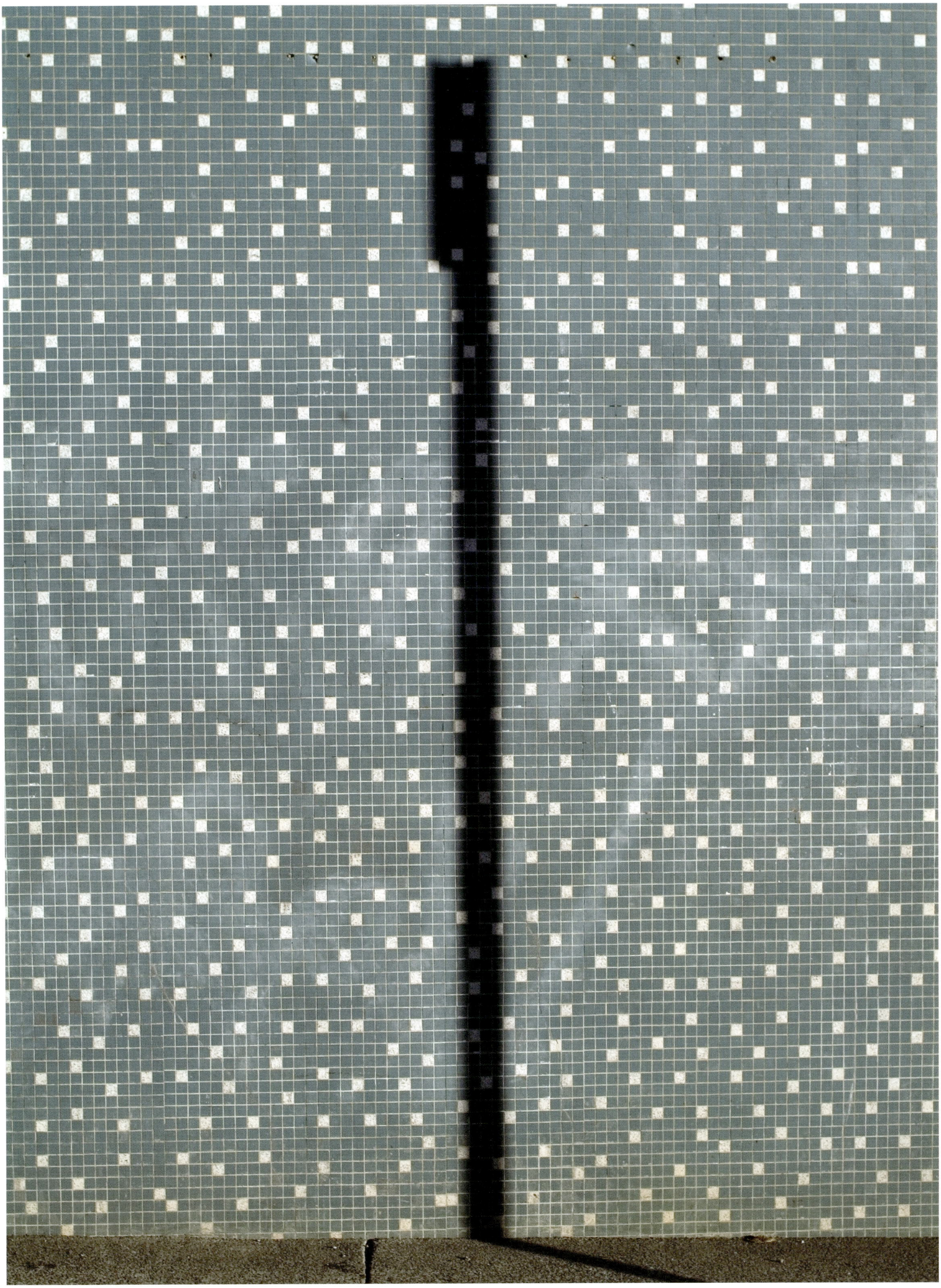

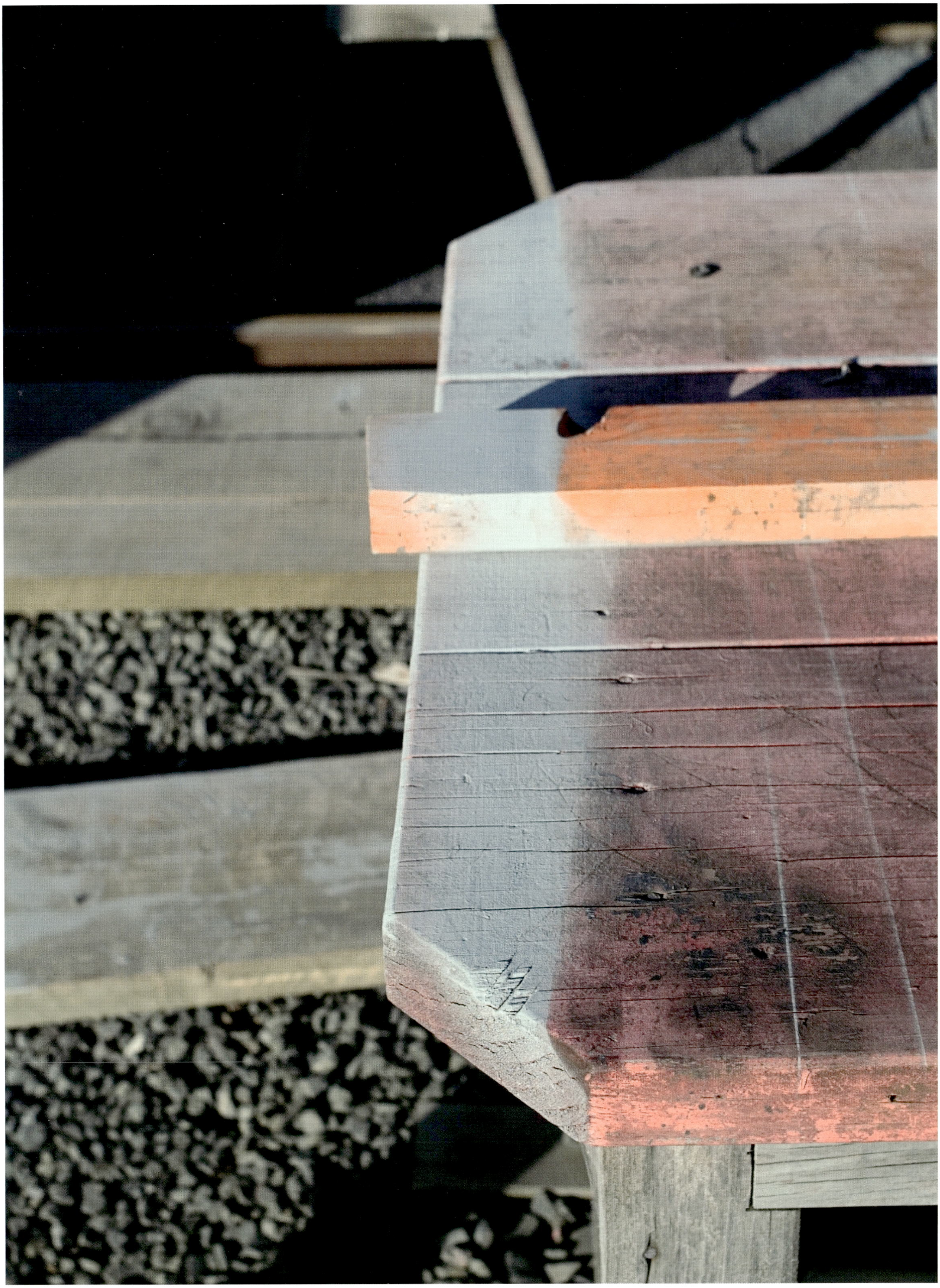

03

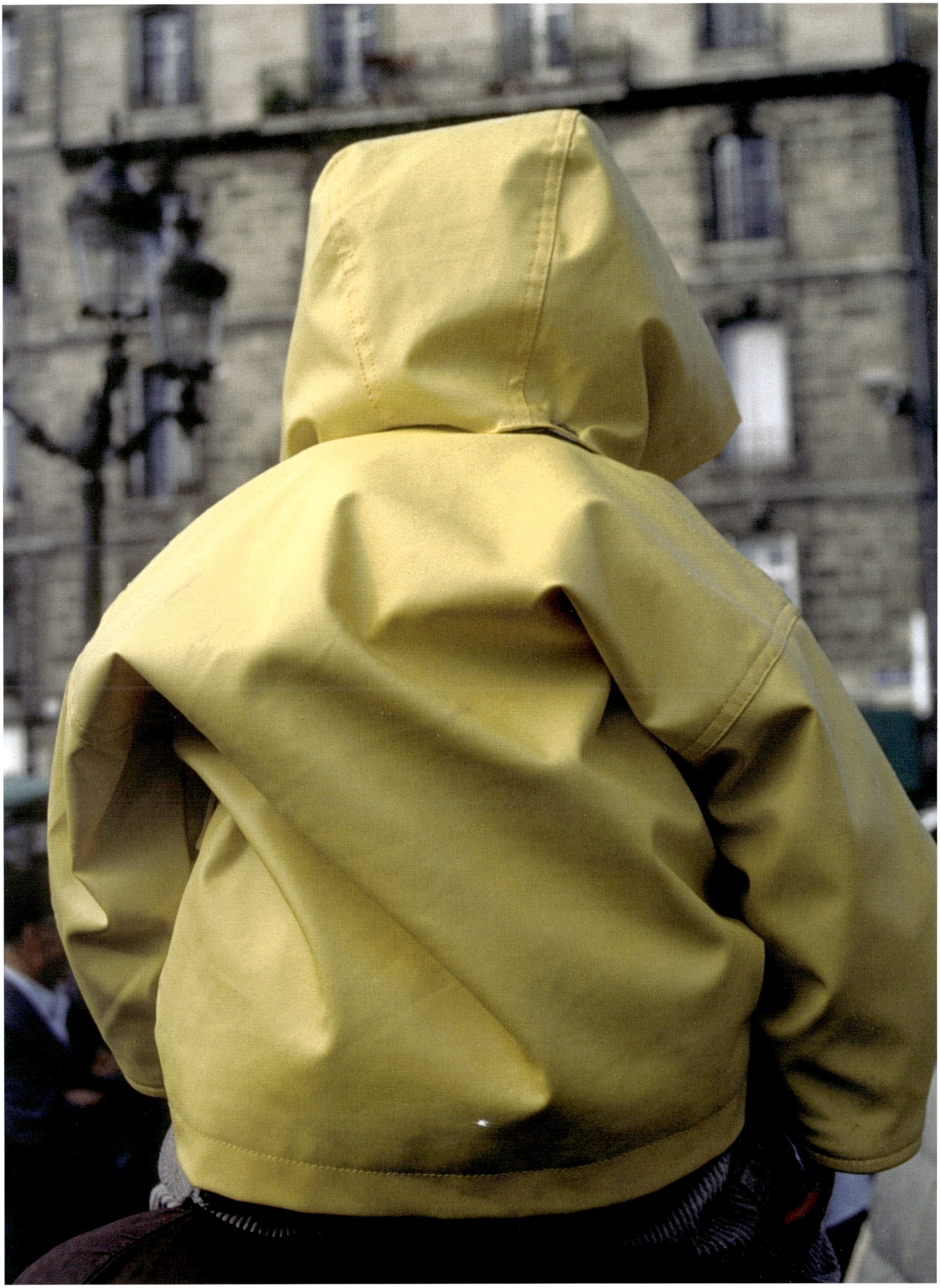

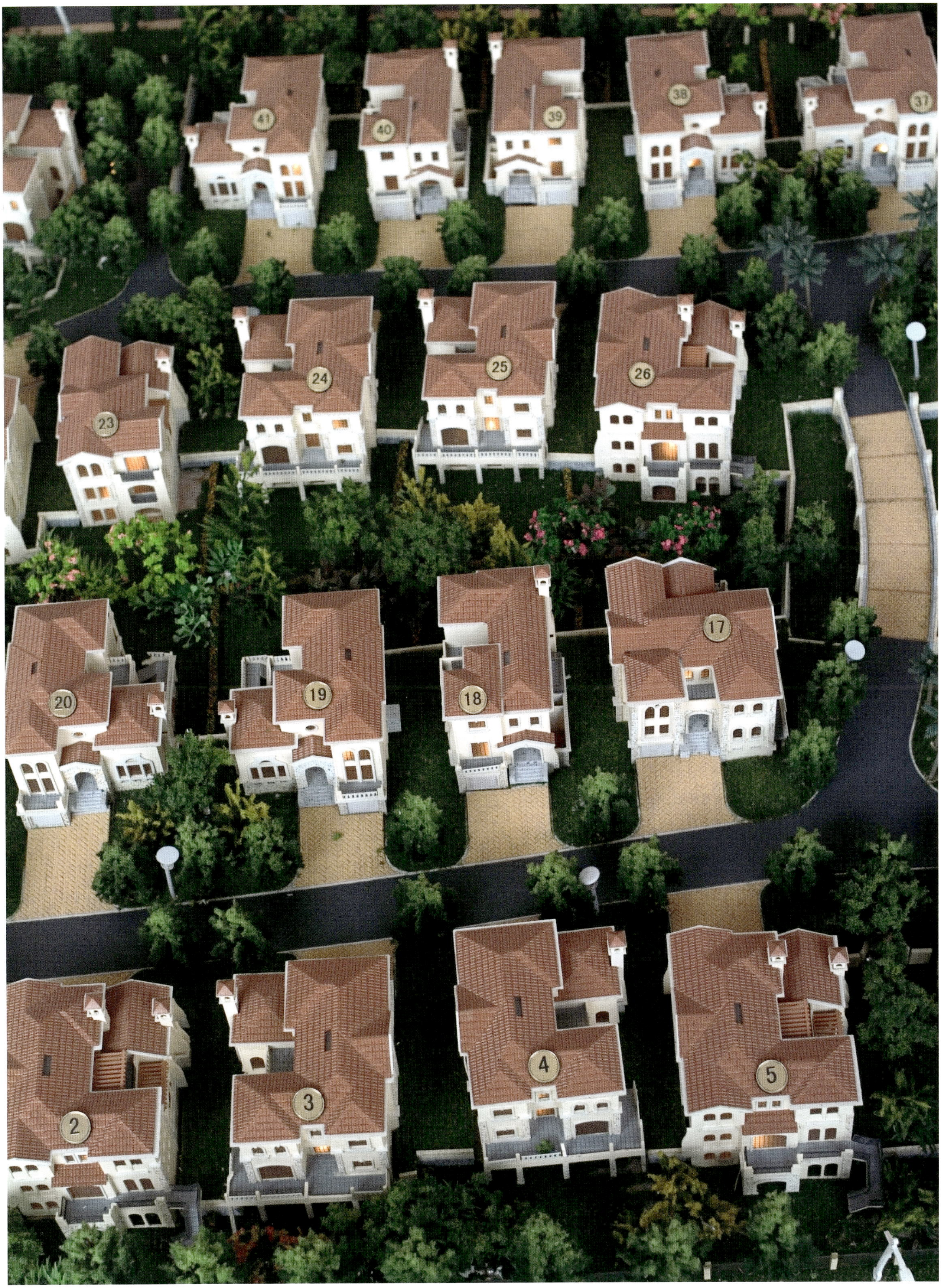
41
40
39
38
37
23
24
25
26
20
19
18
17
2
3
4
5

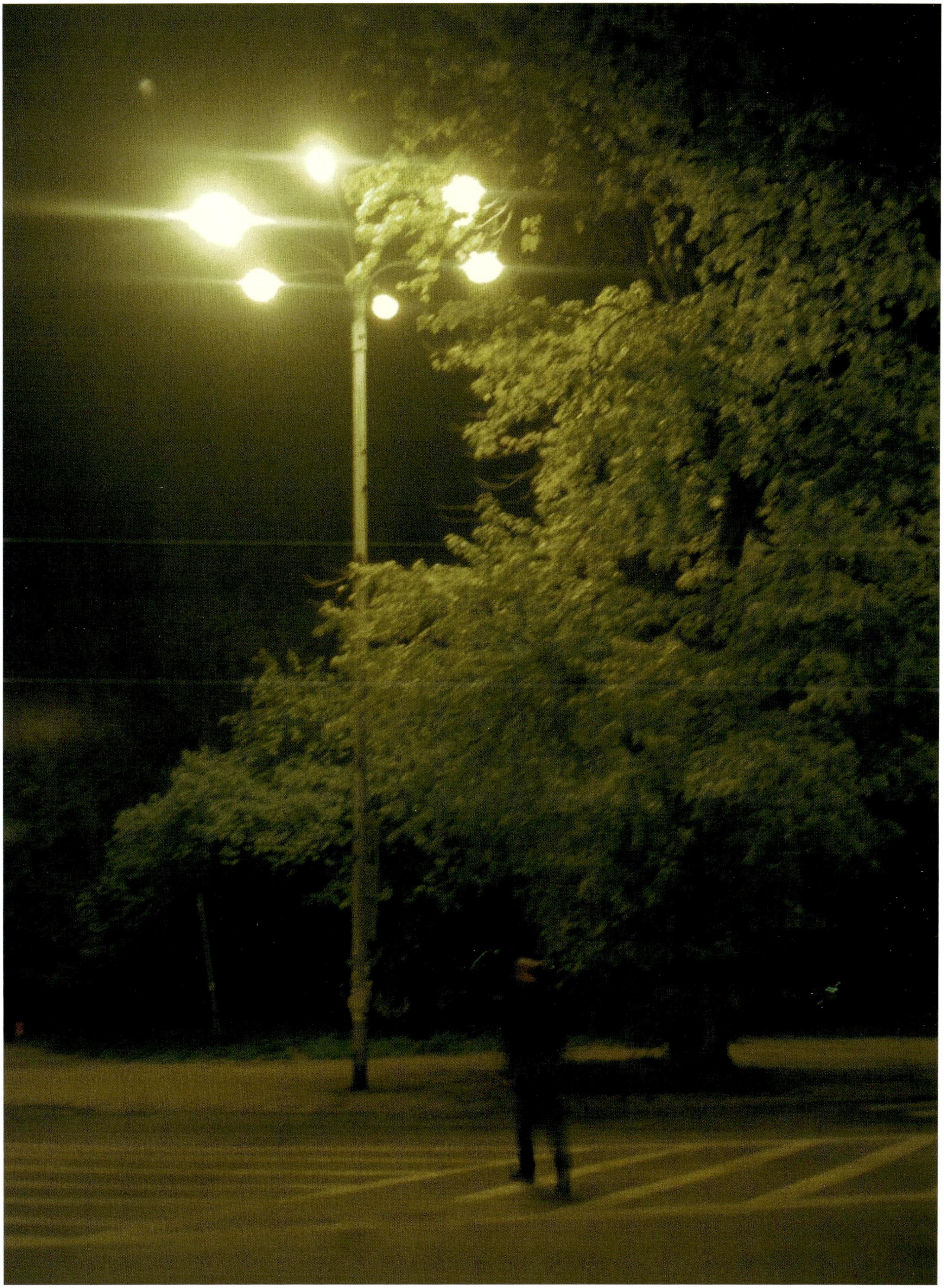

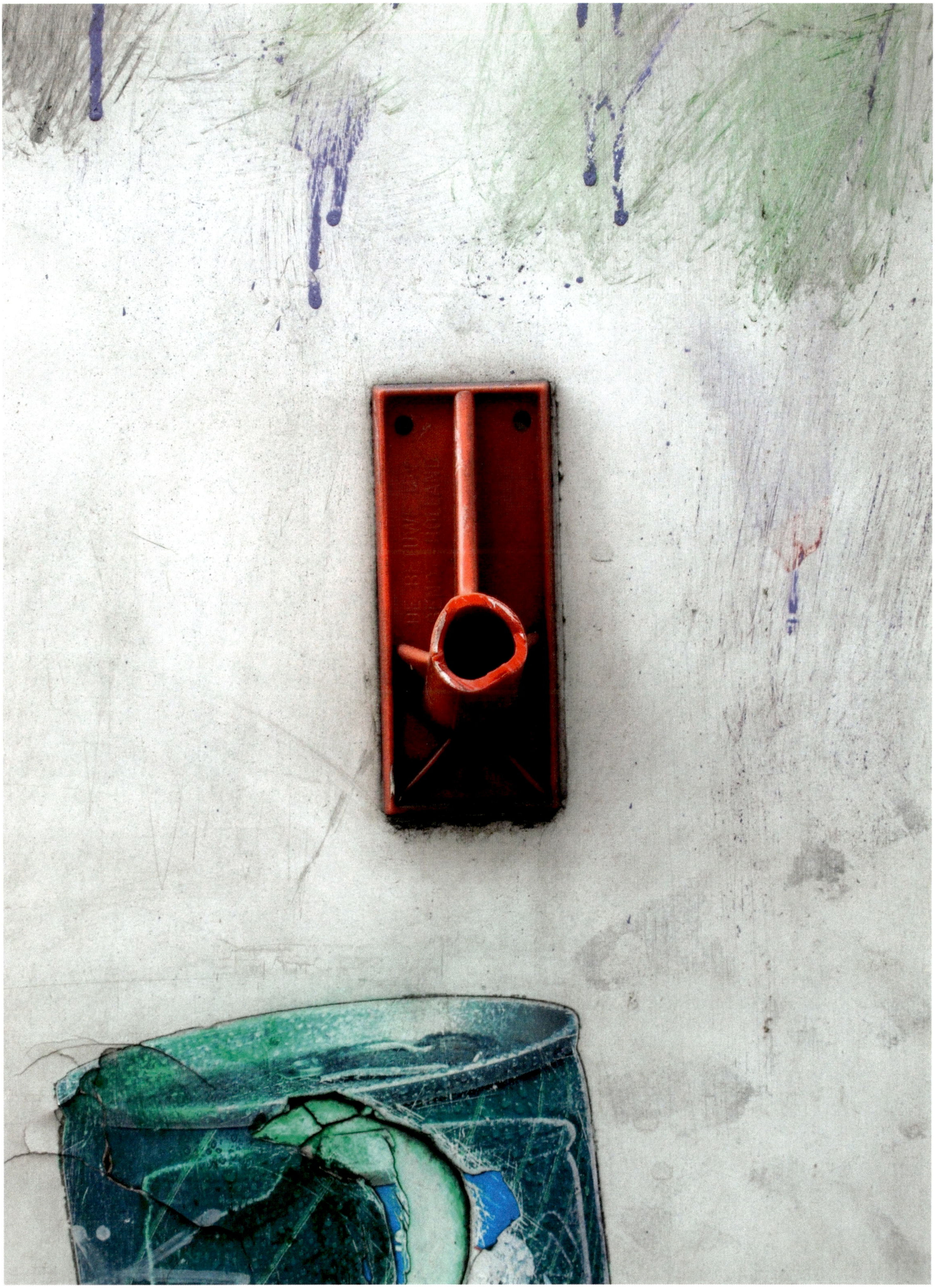

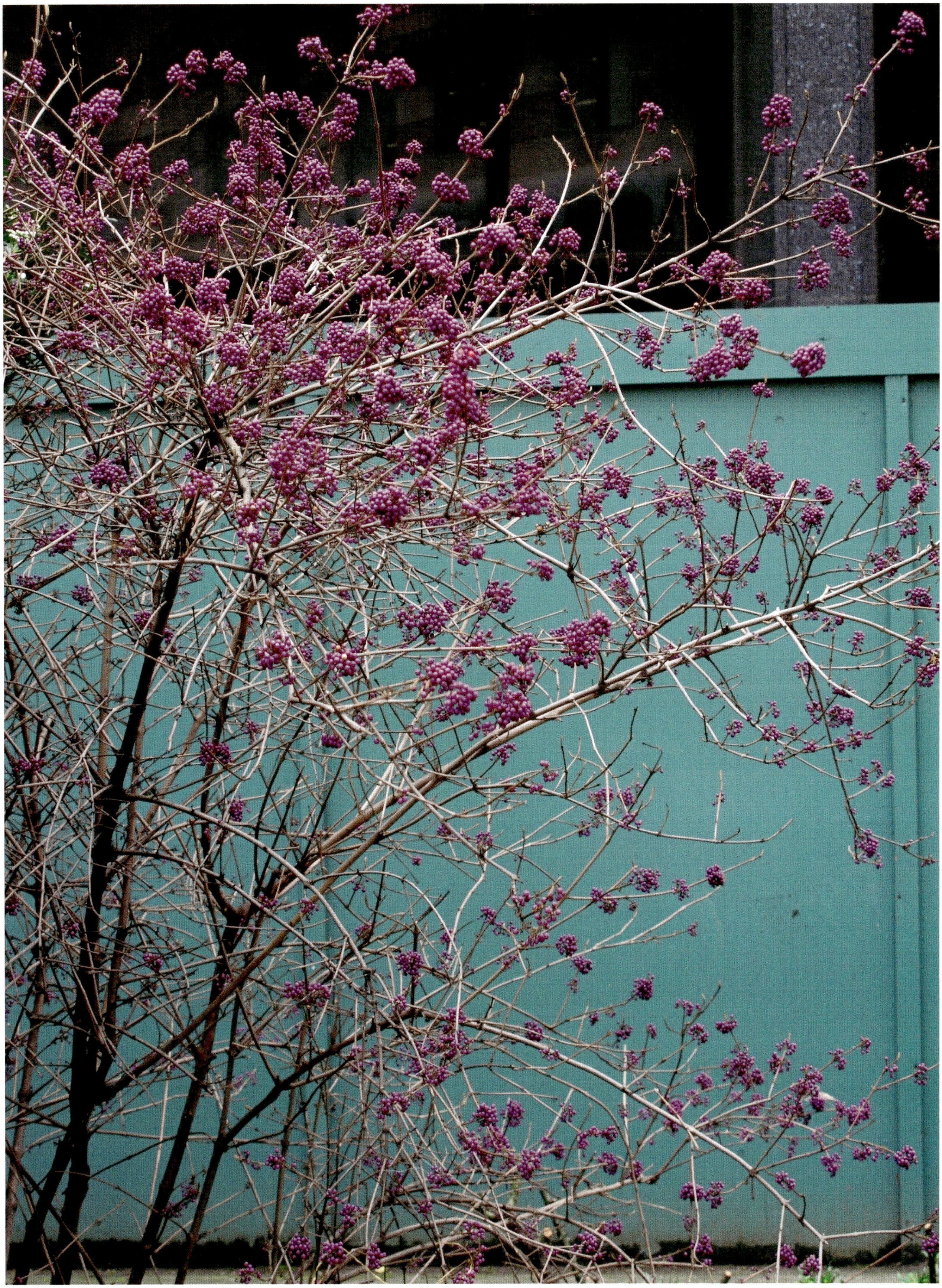

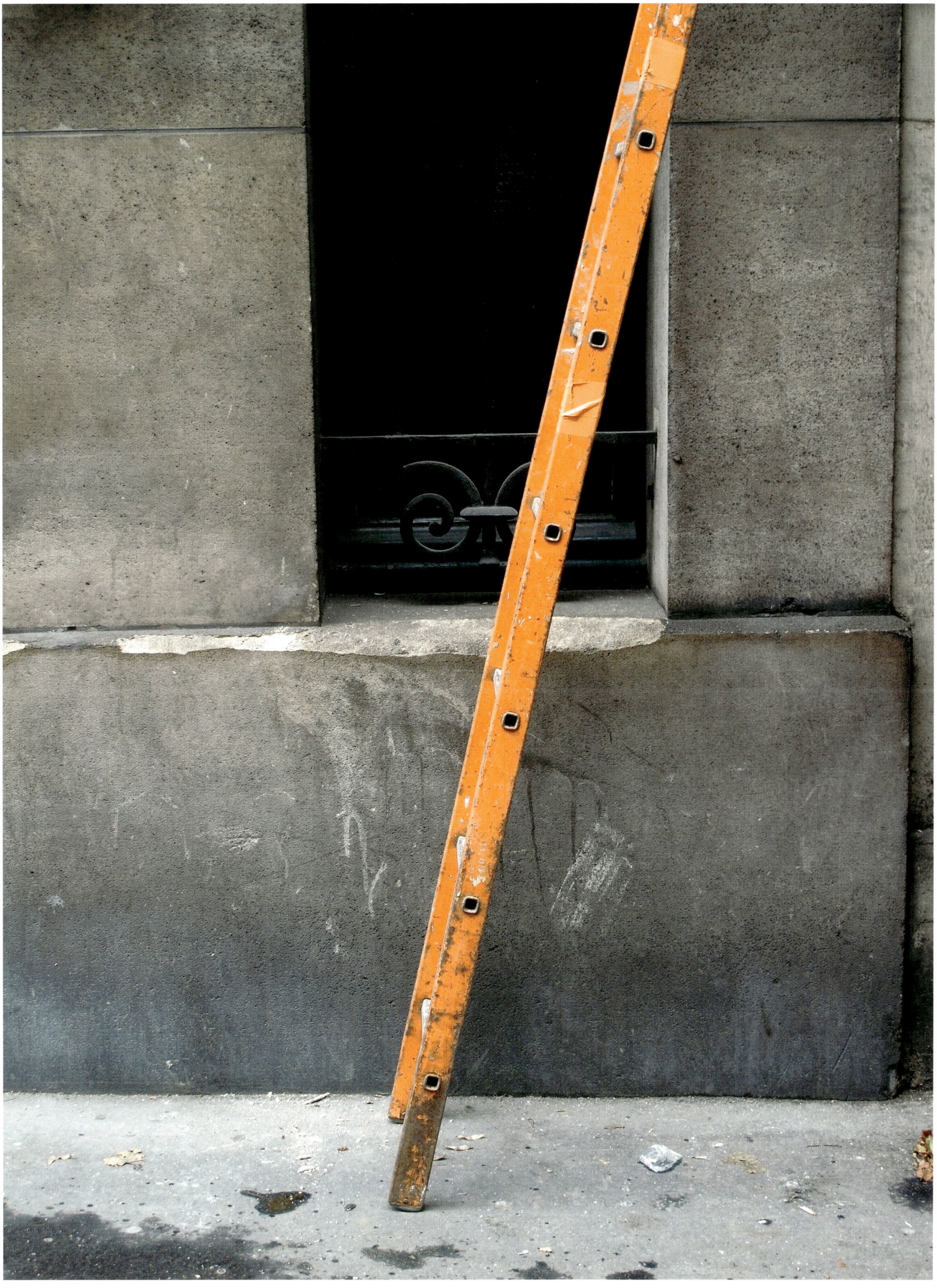

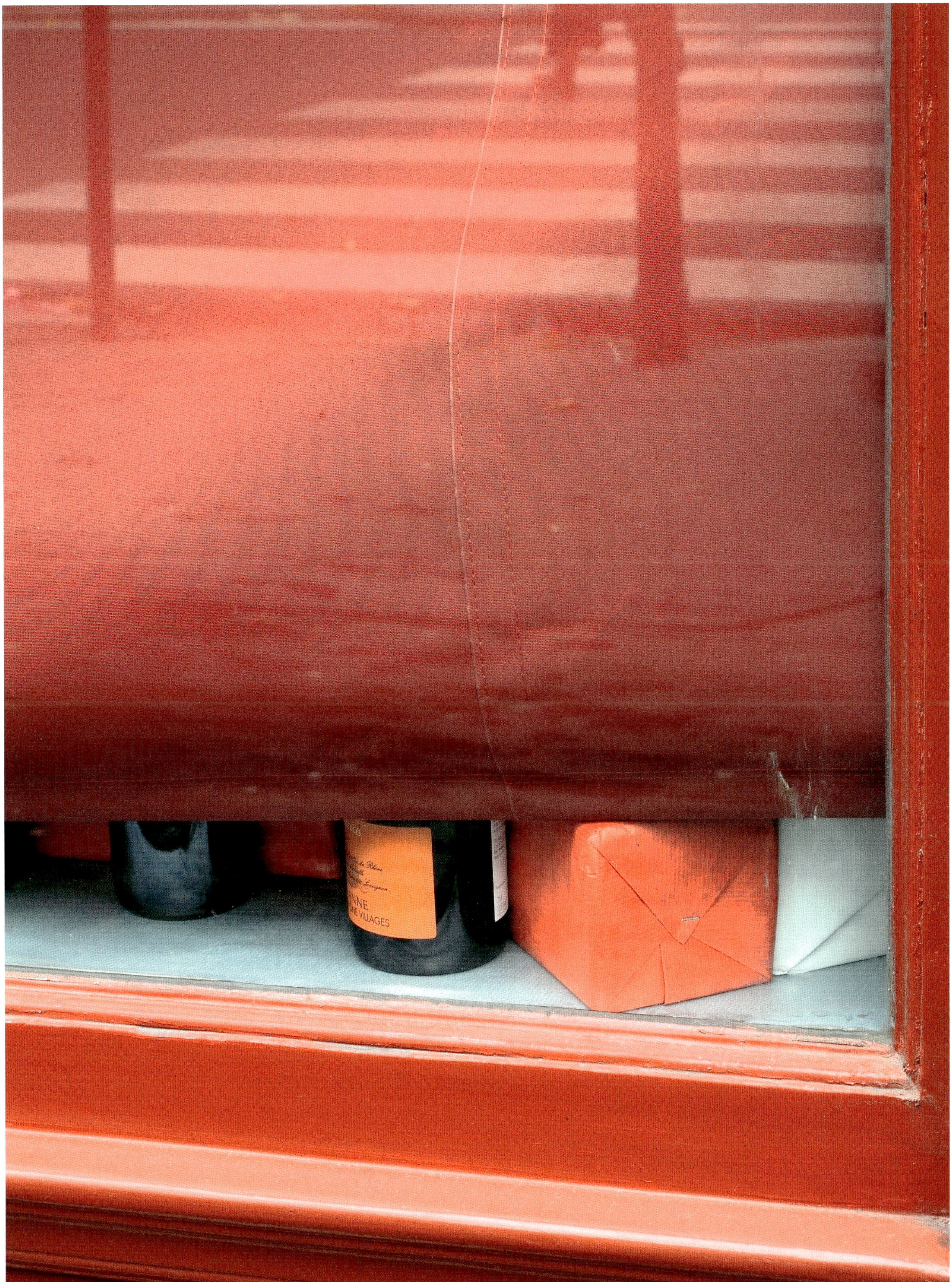

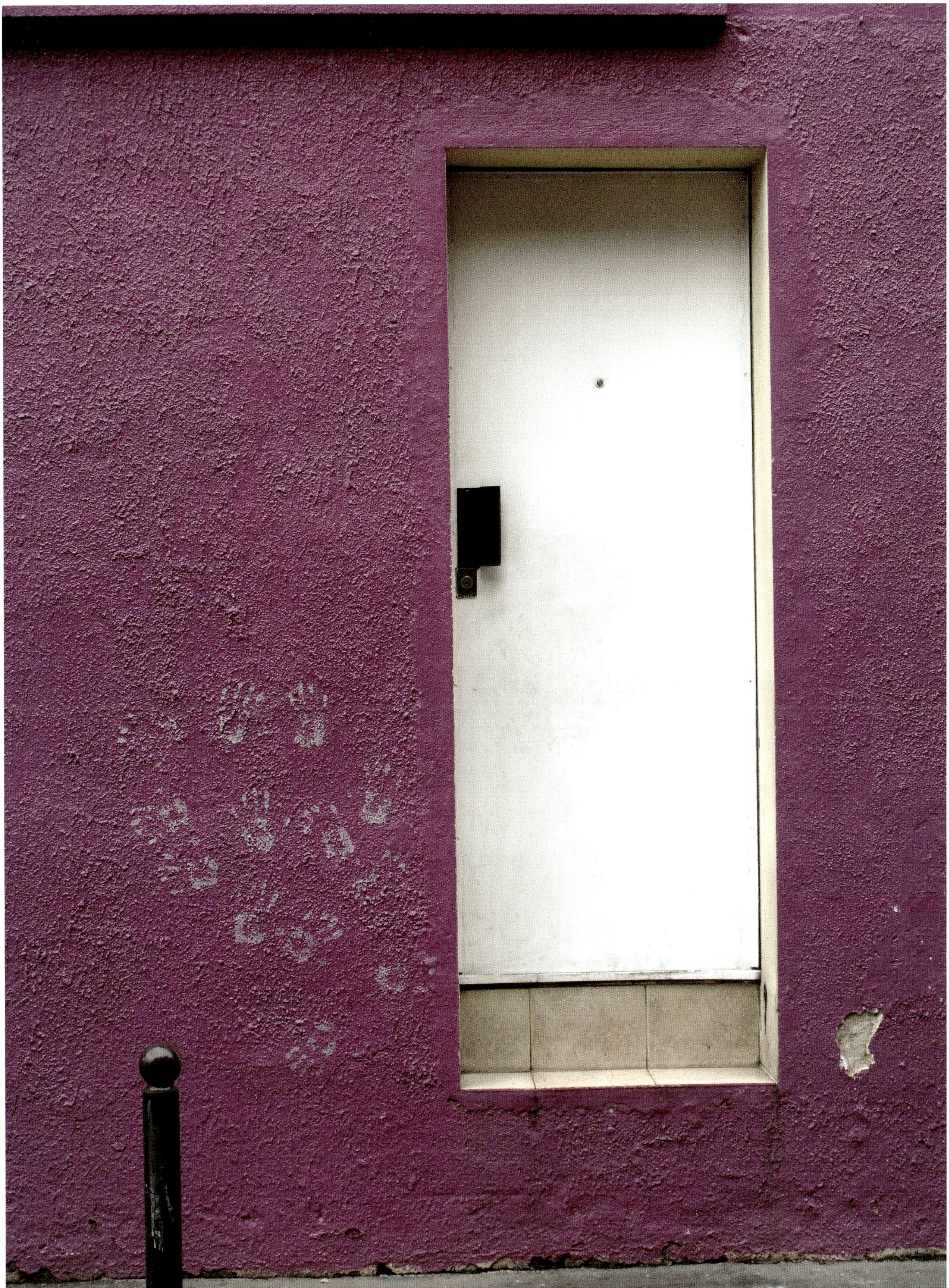

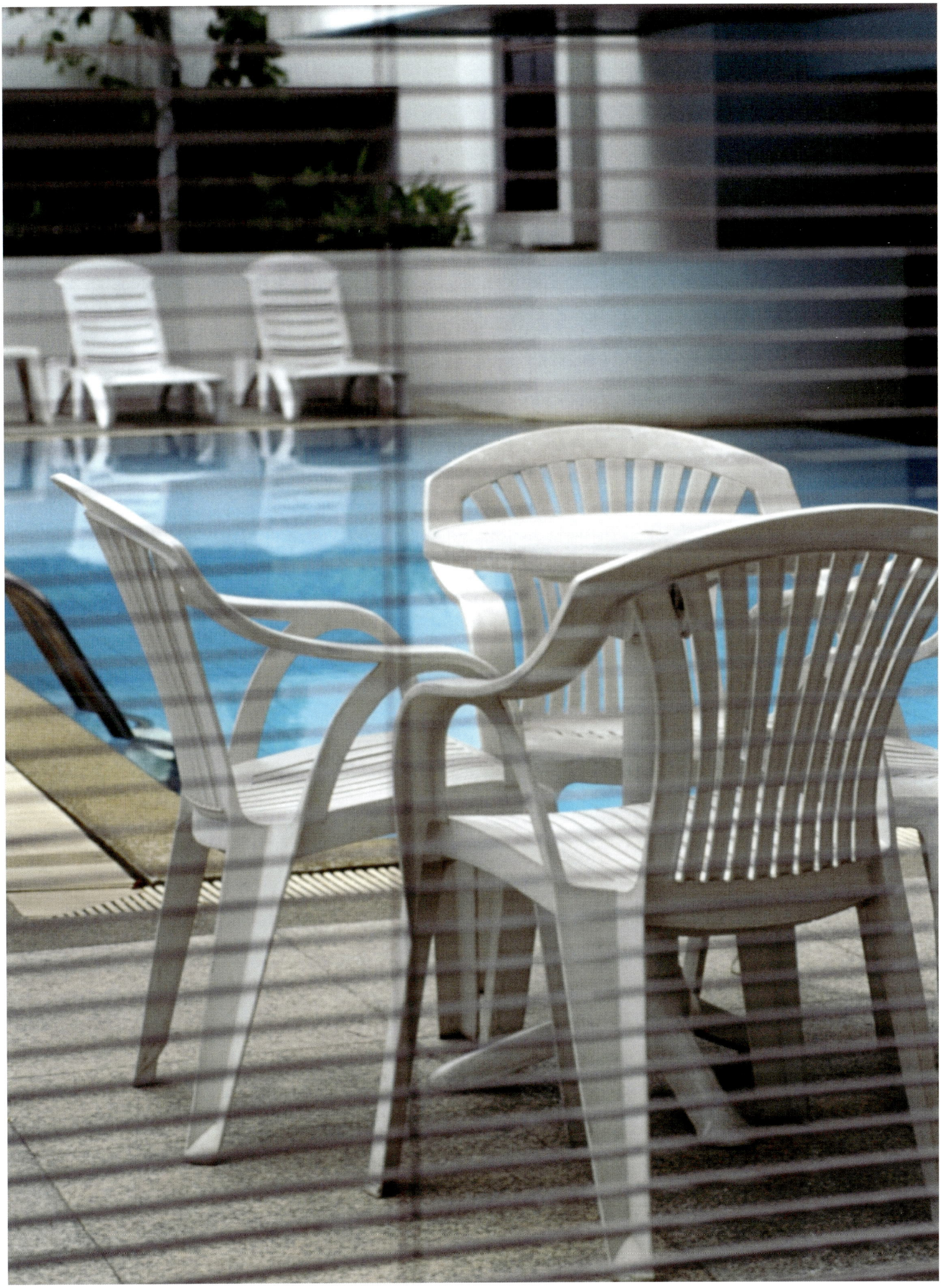

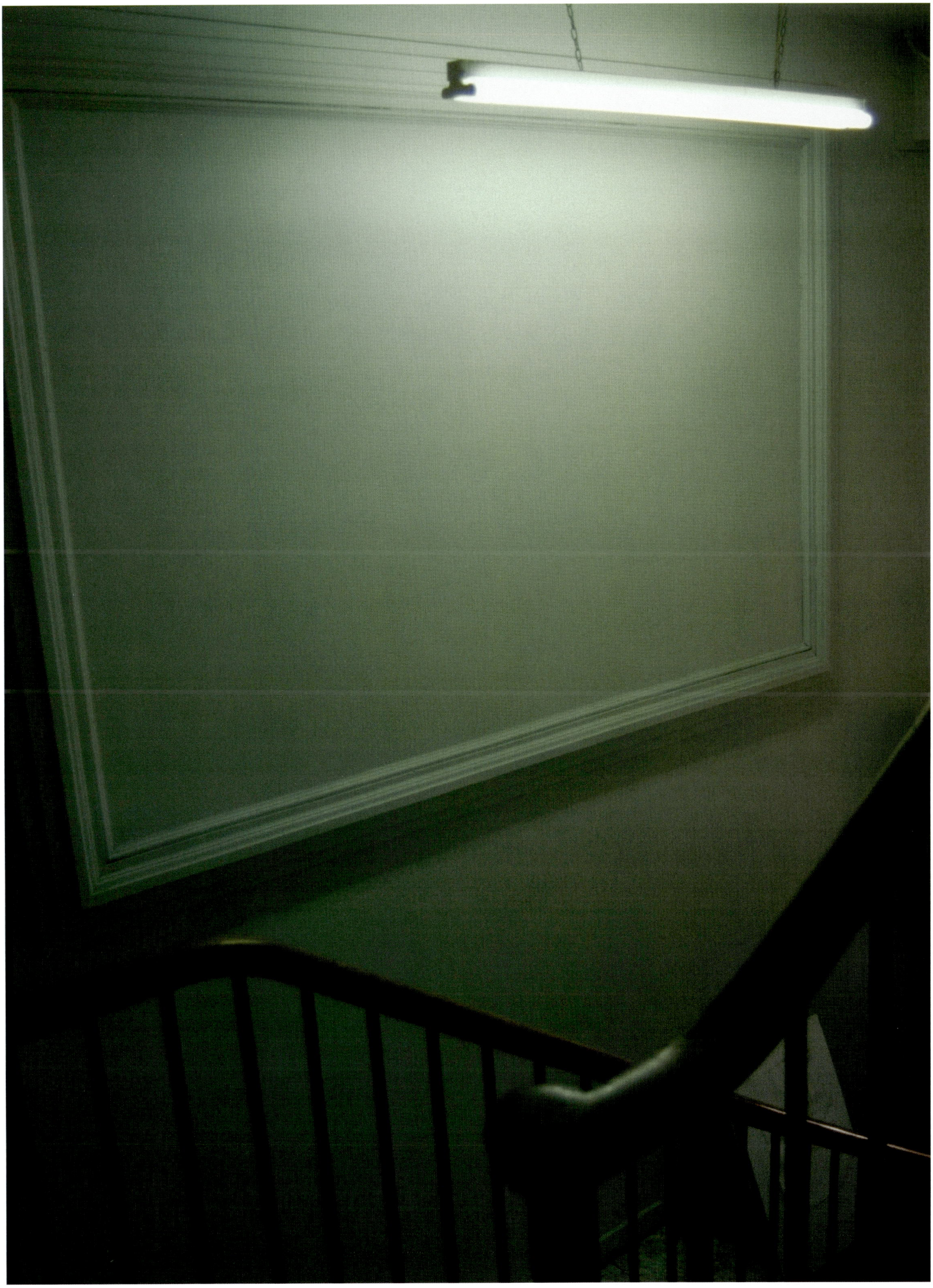

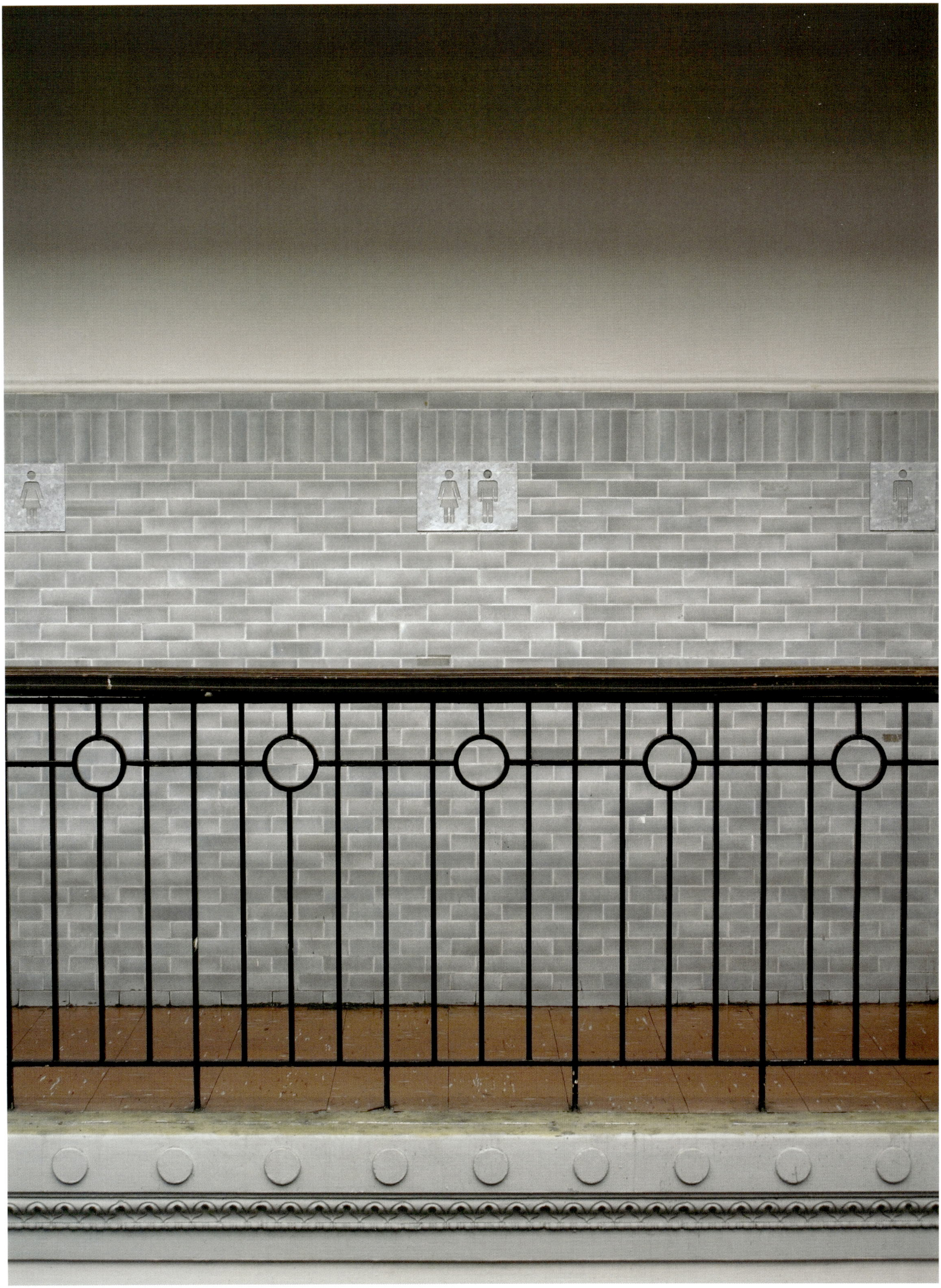

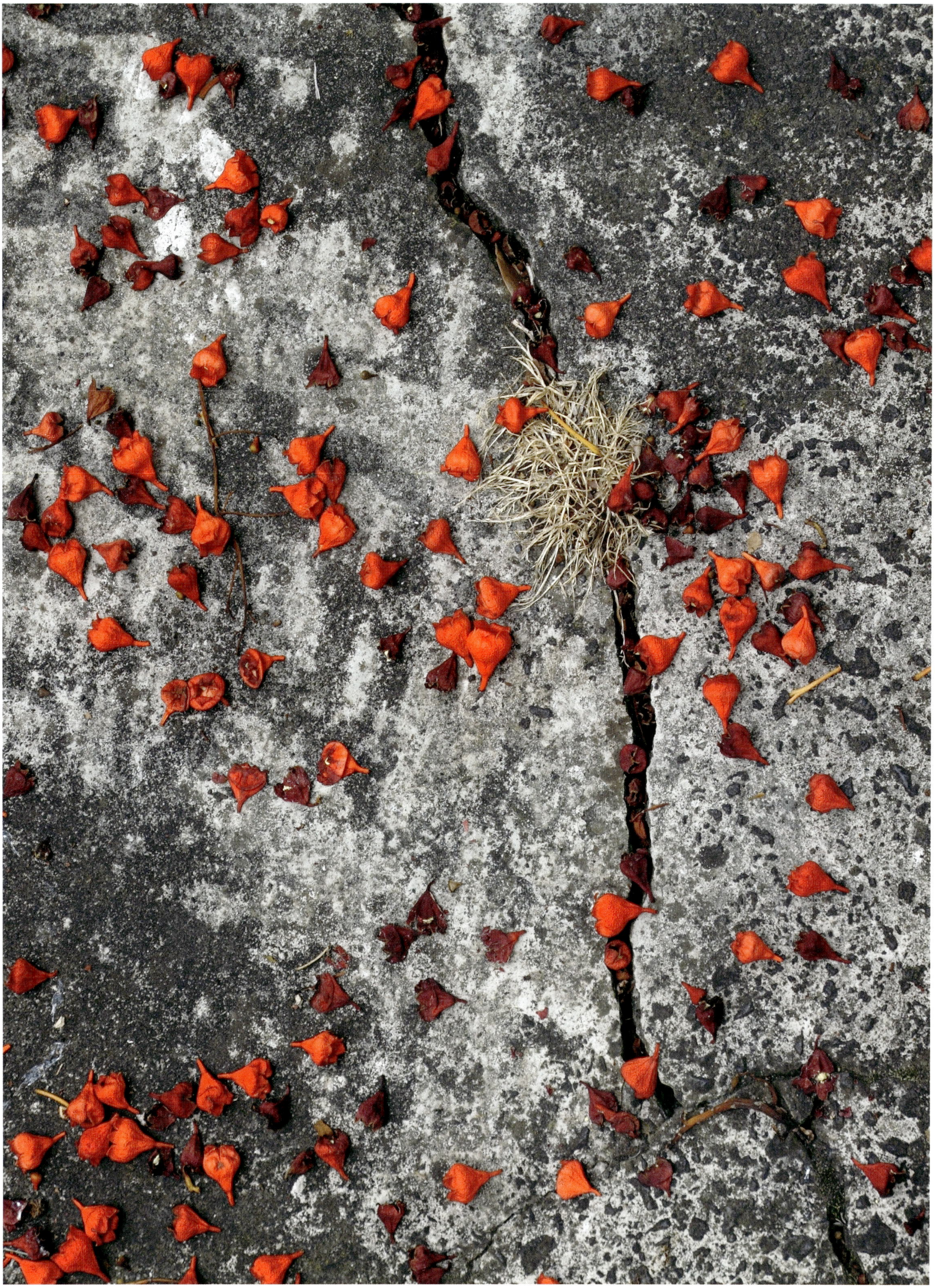

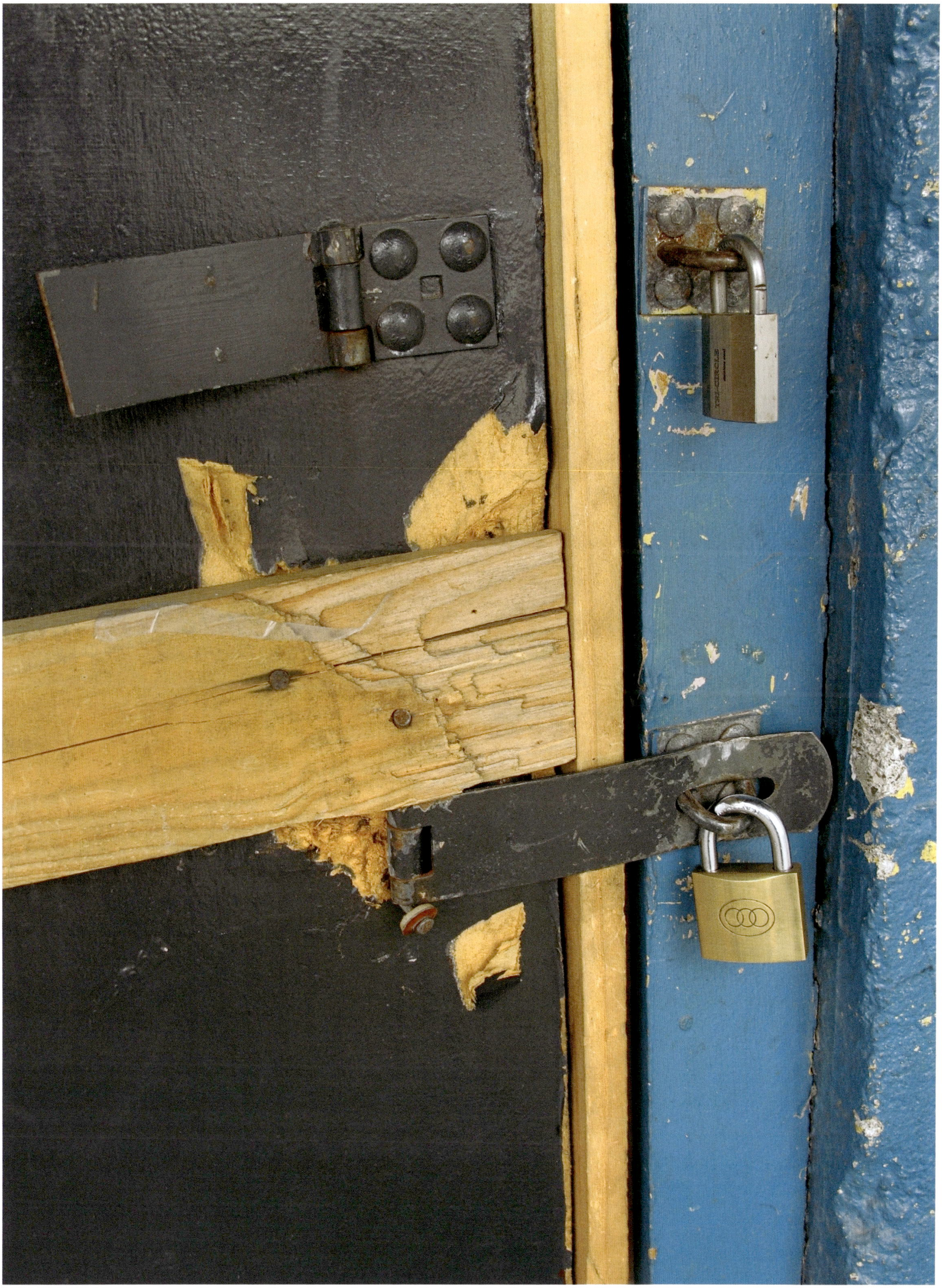

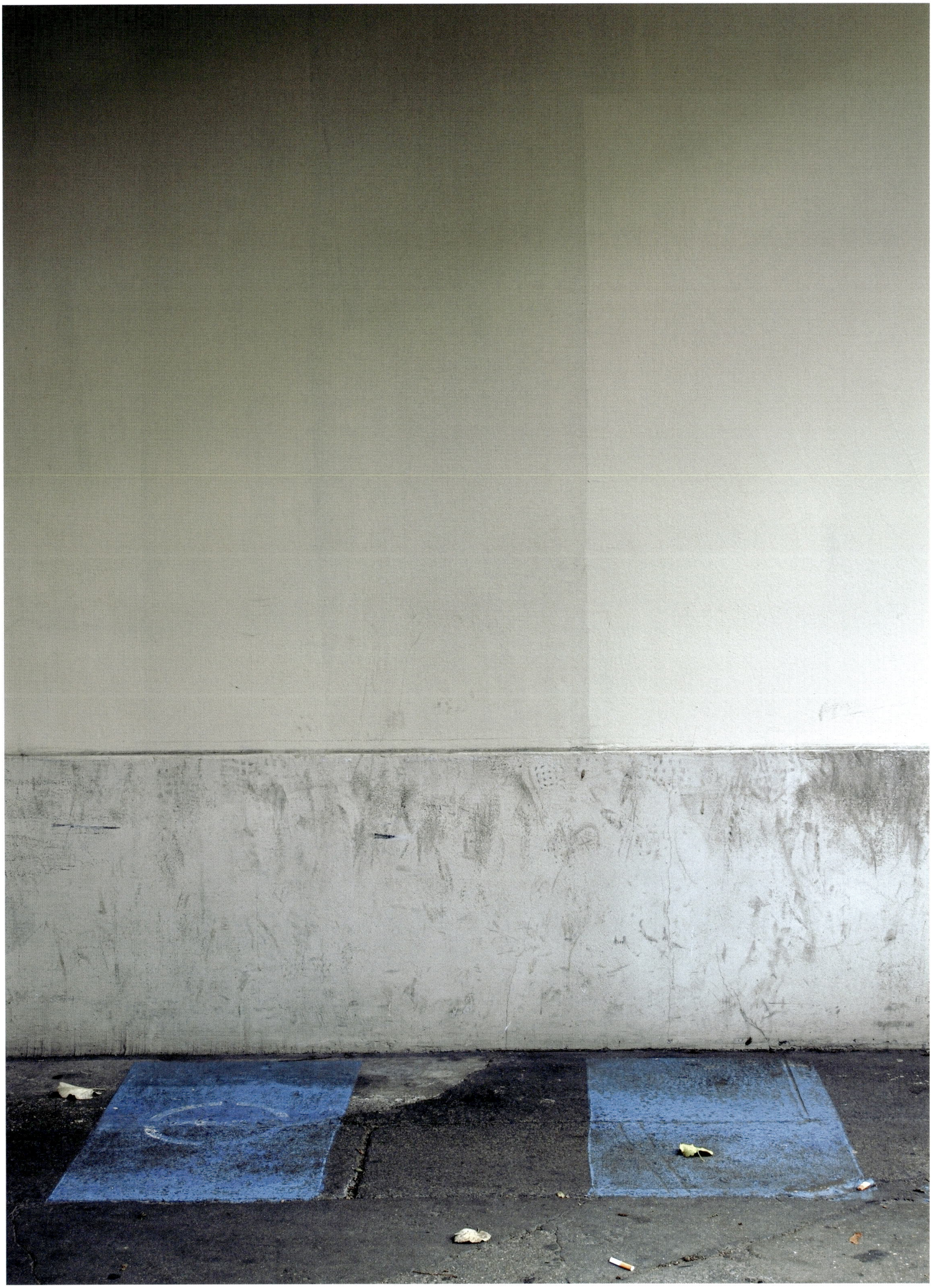

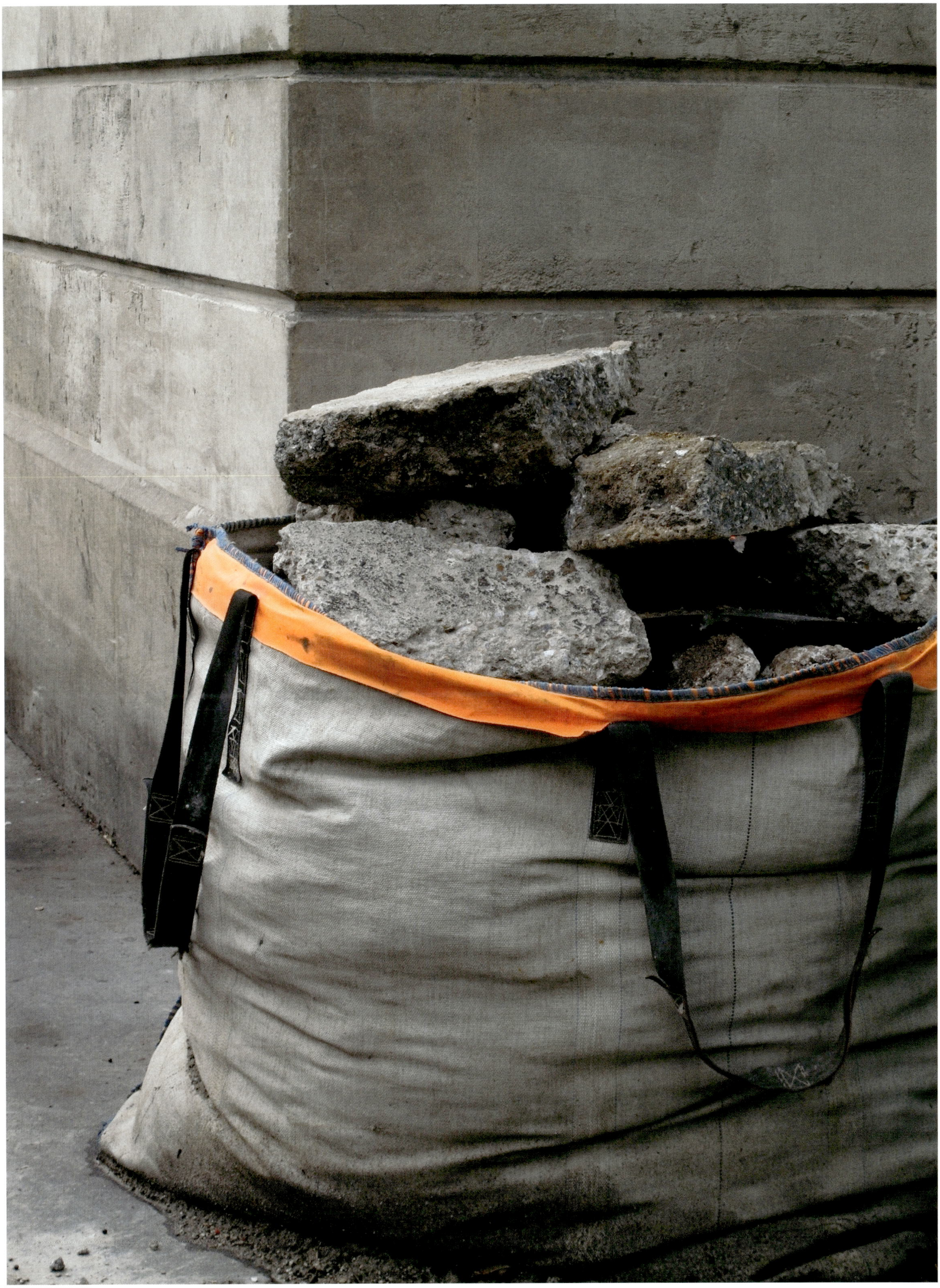

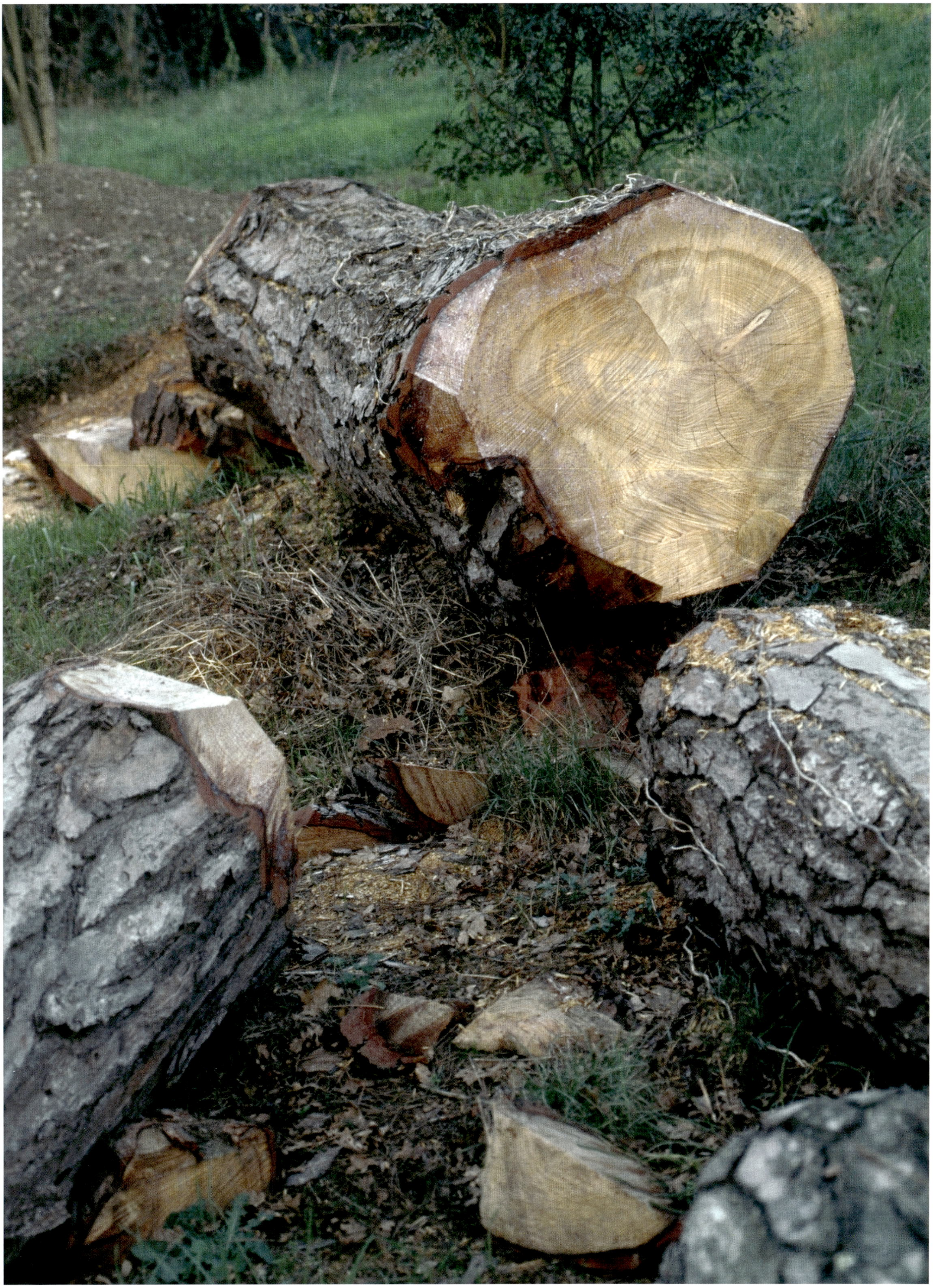

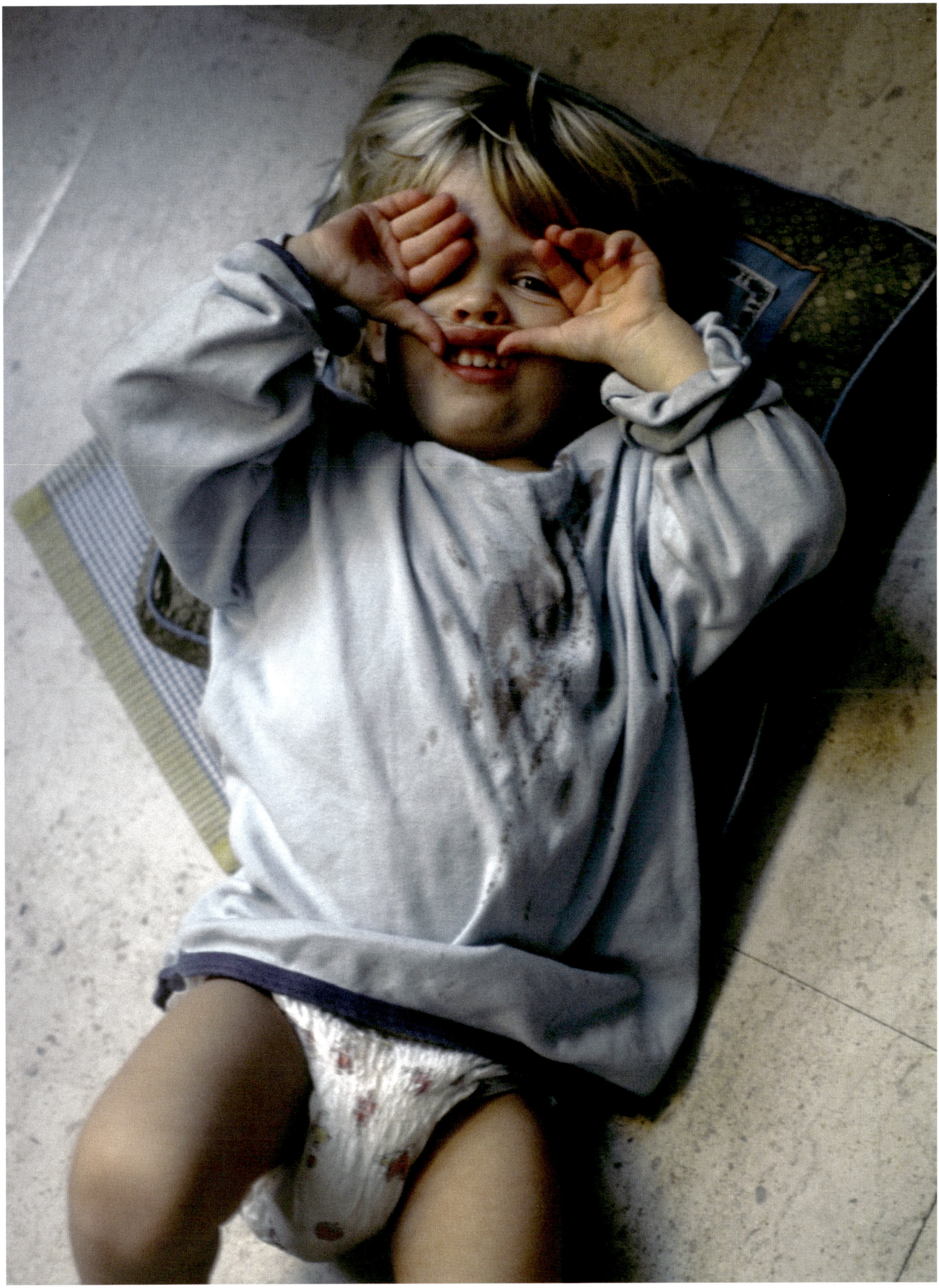

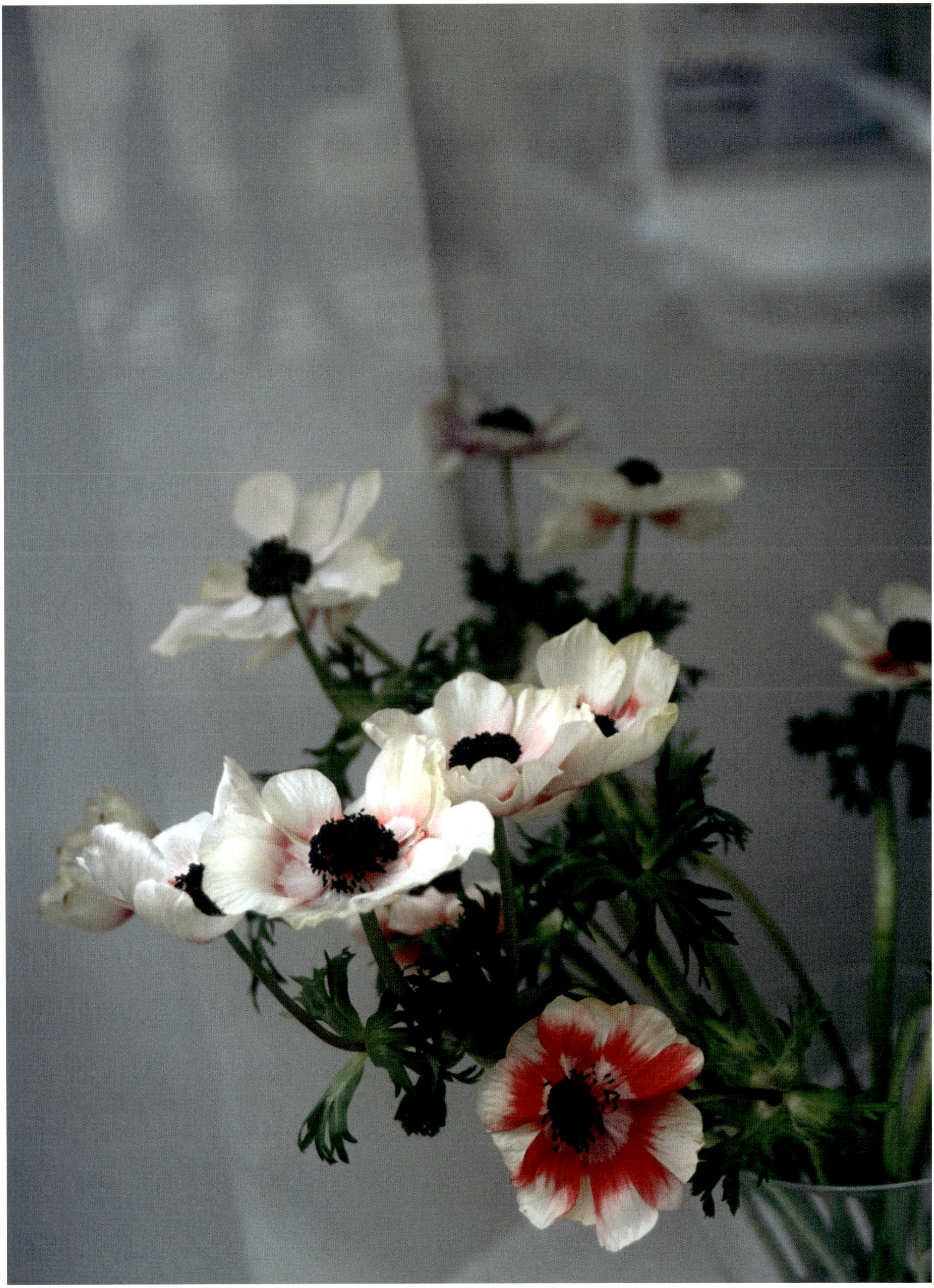

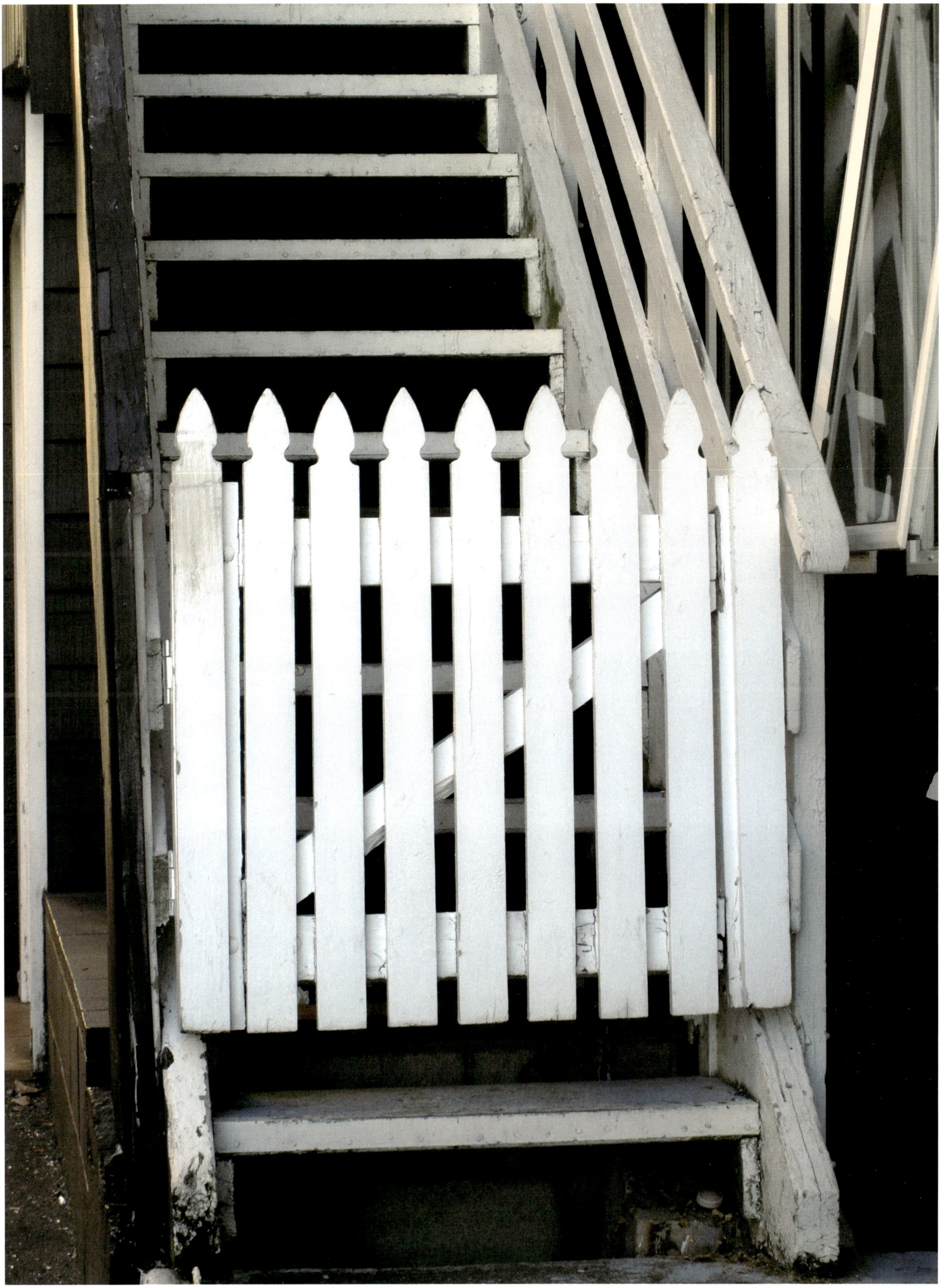

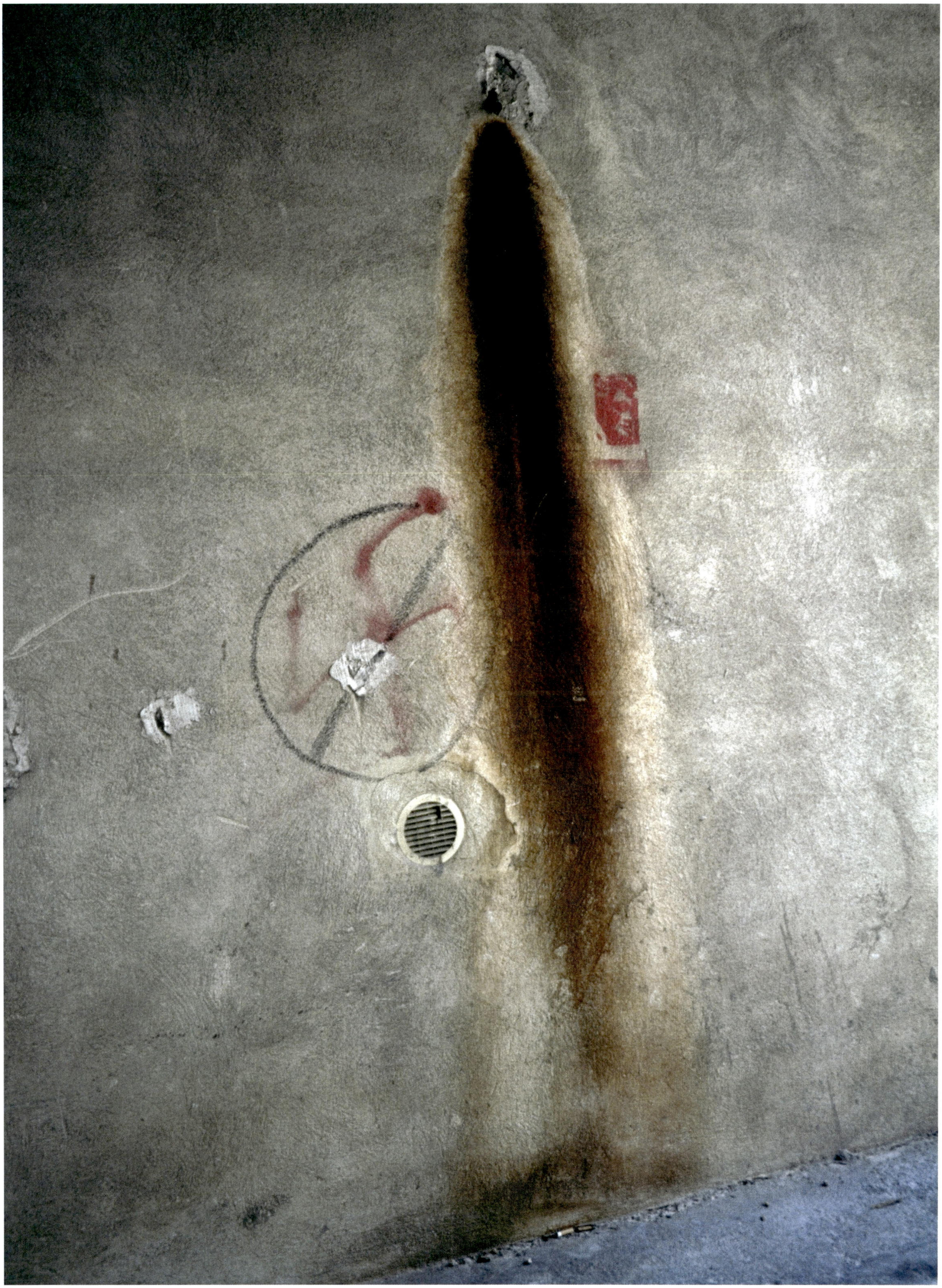

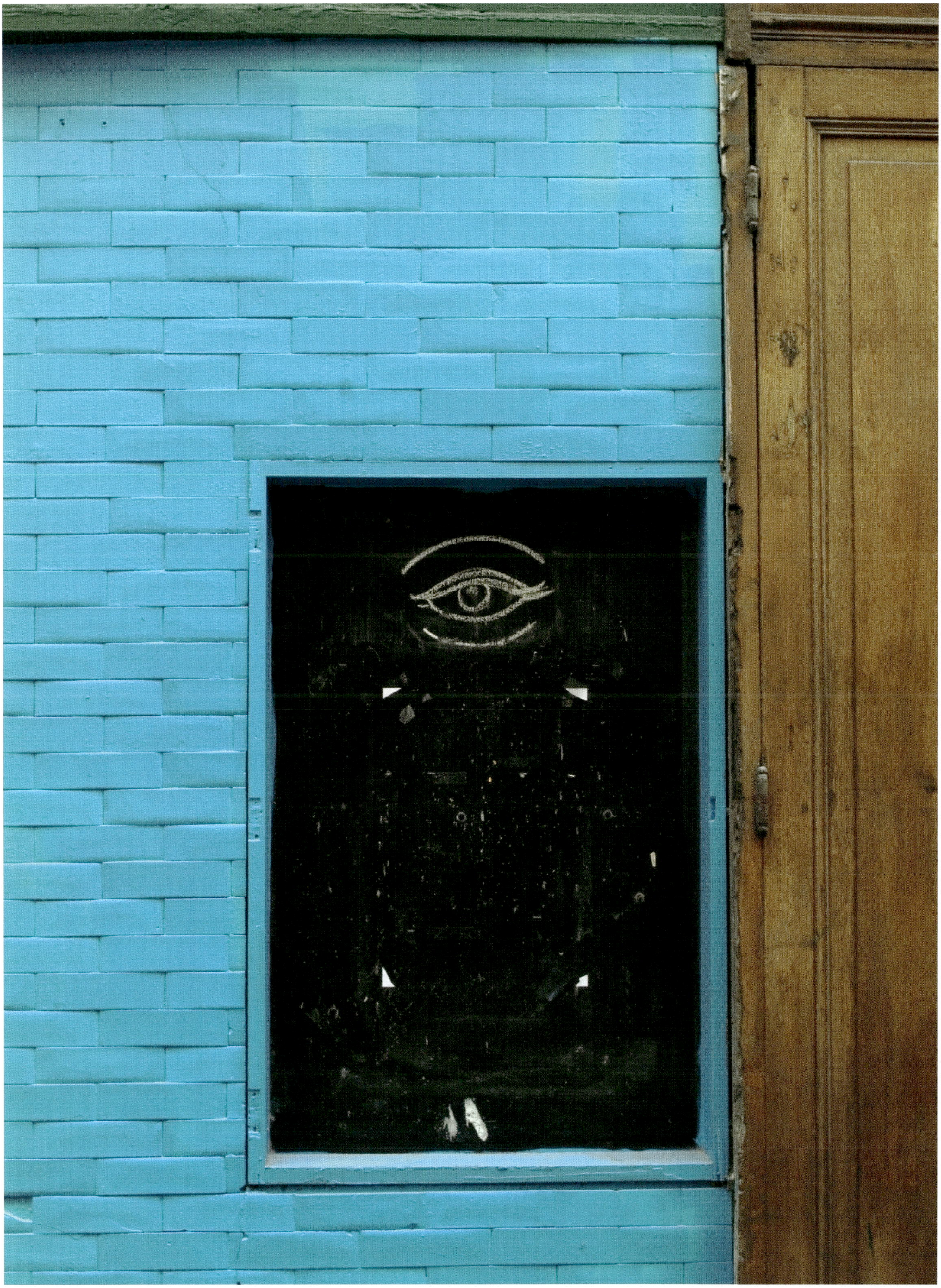

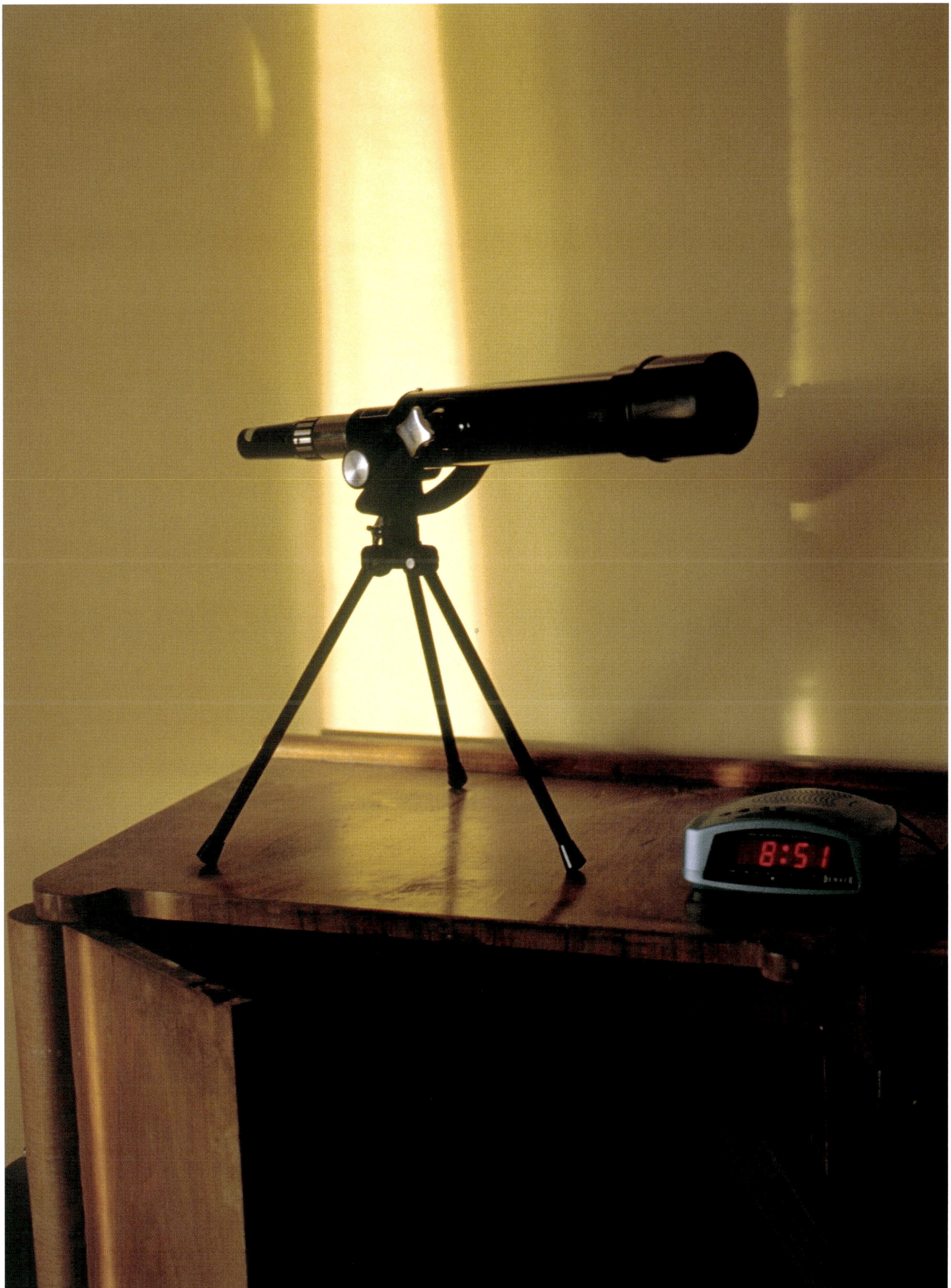
8:51

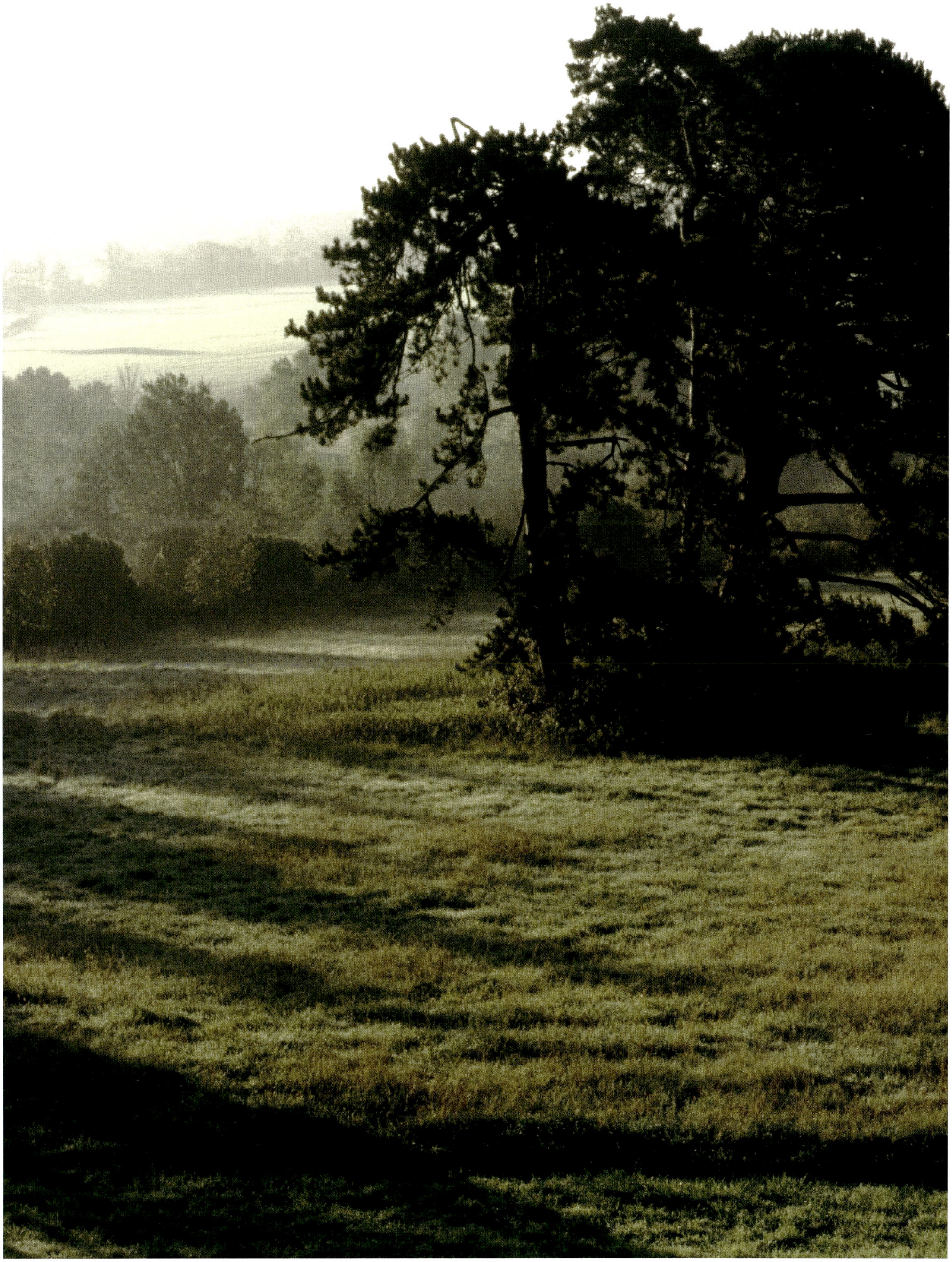

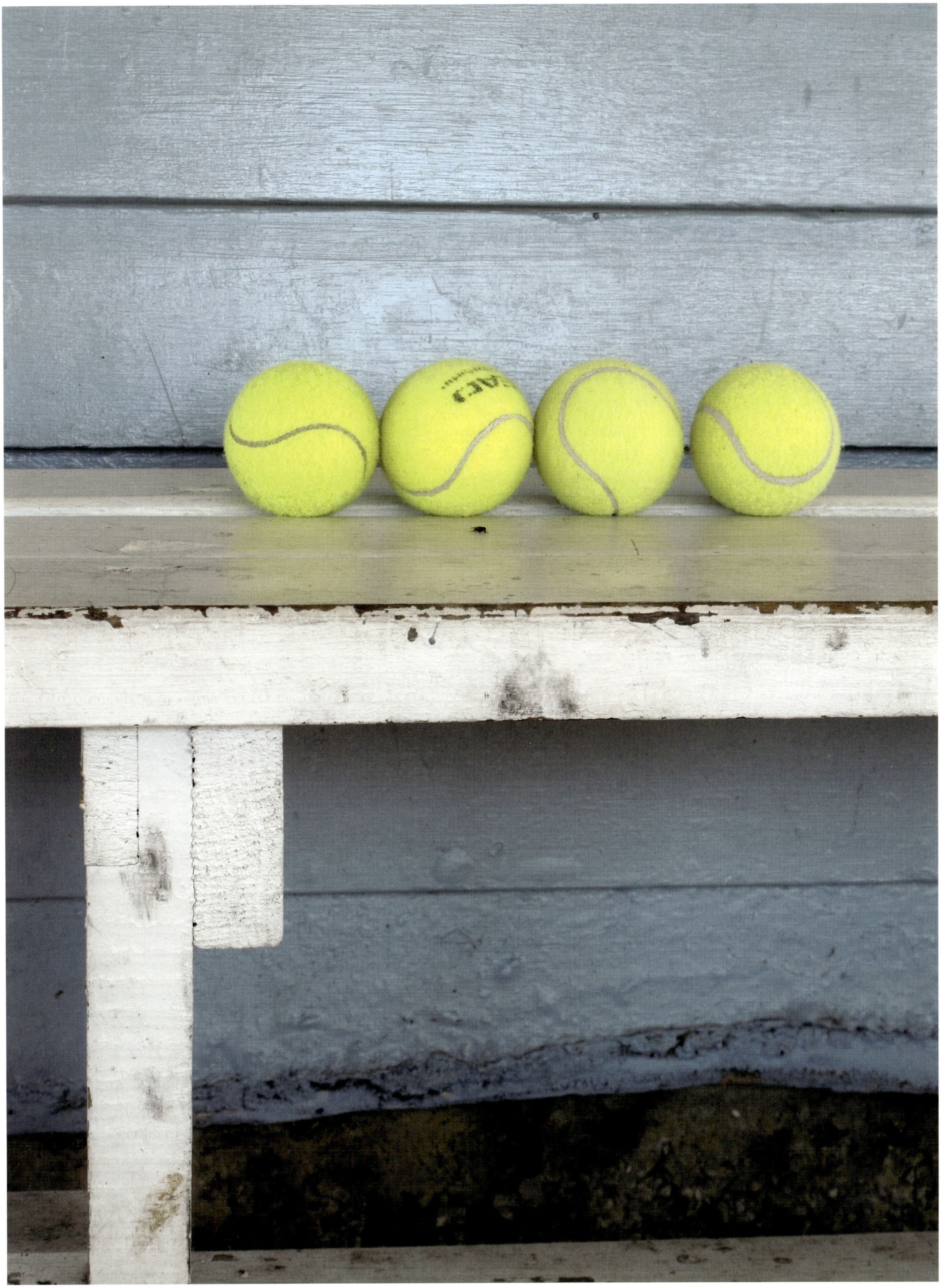

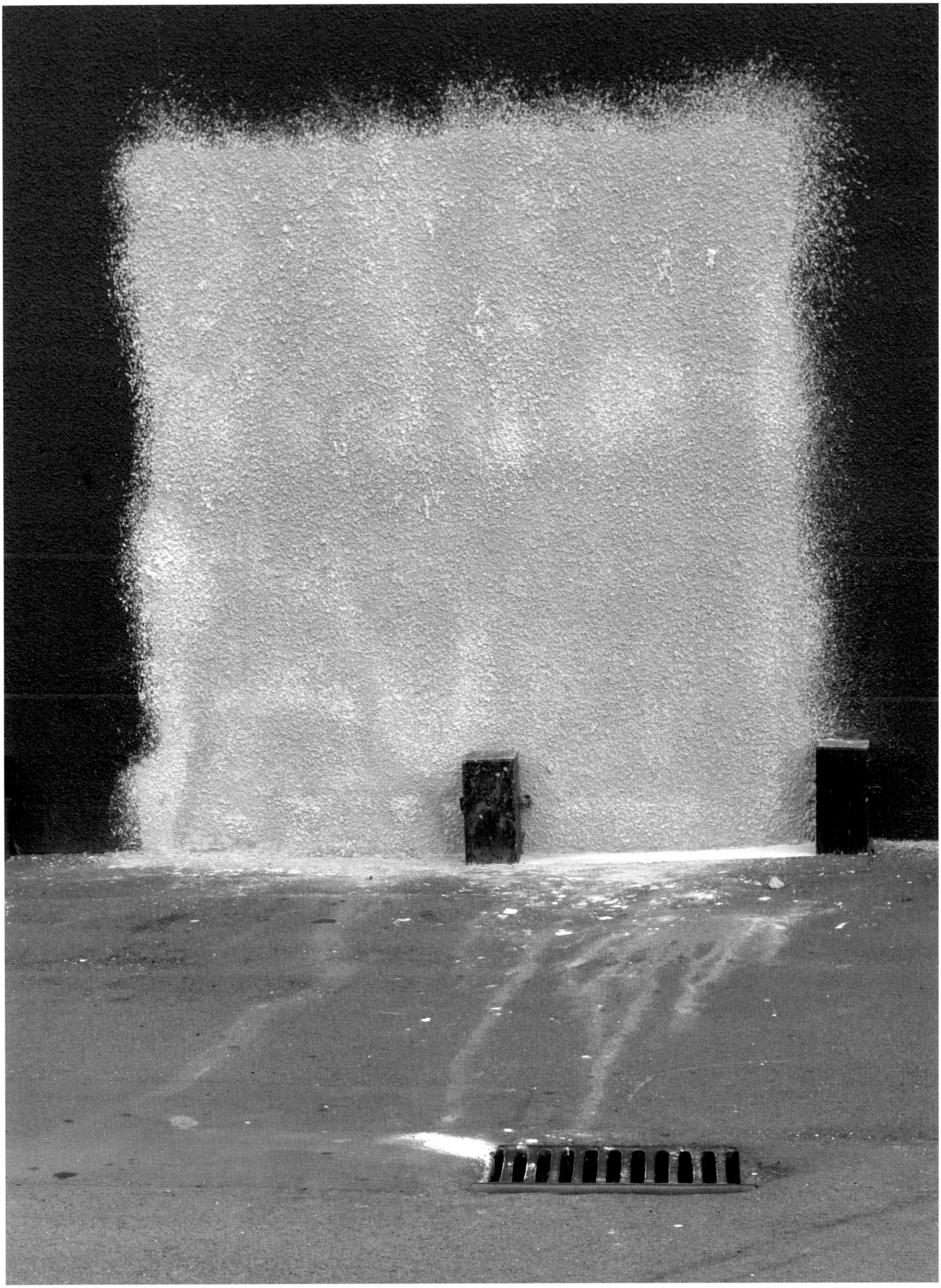

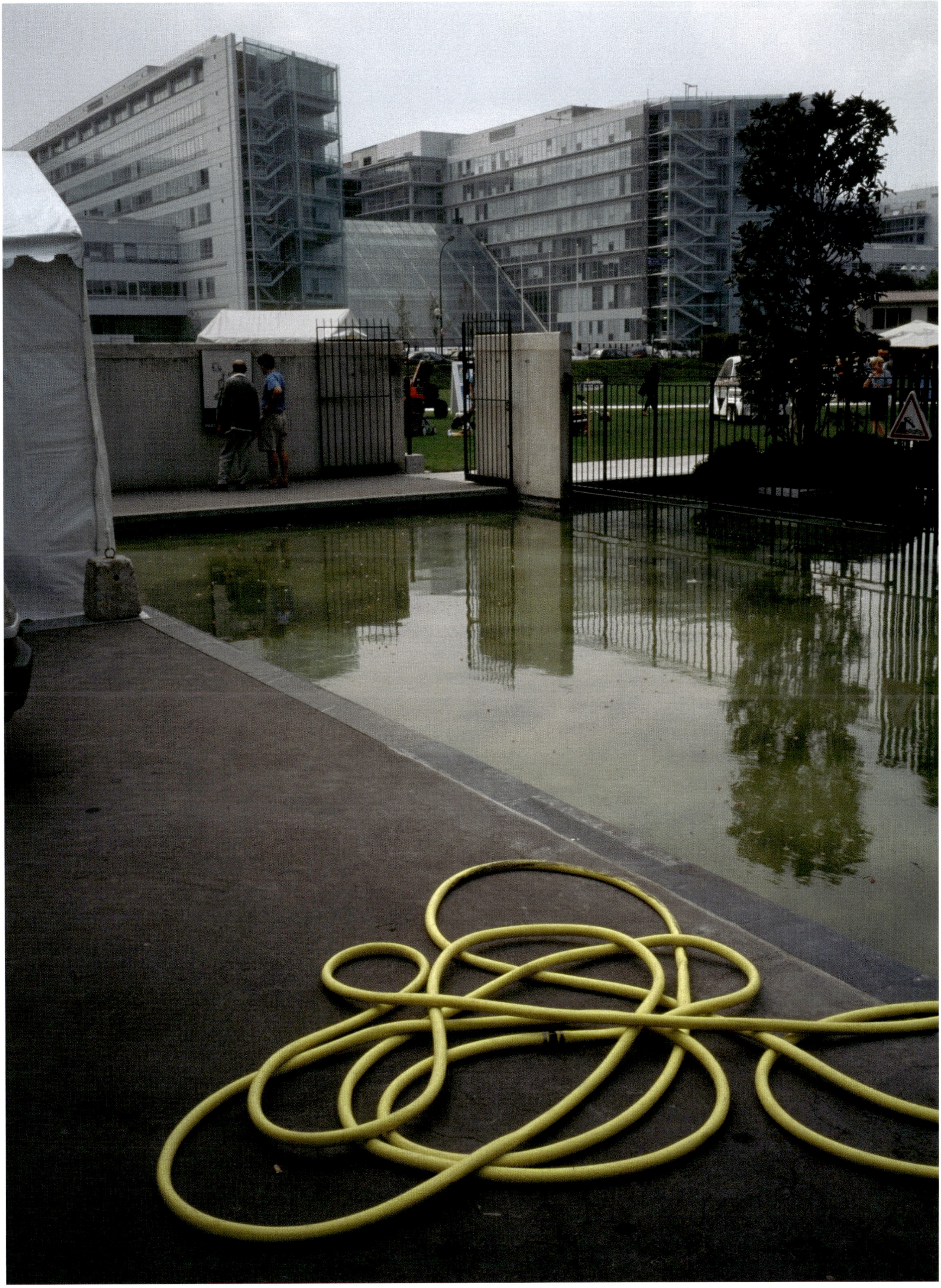

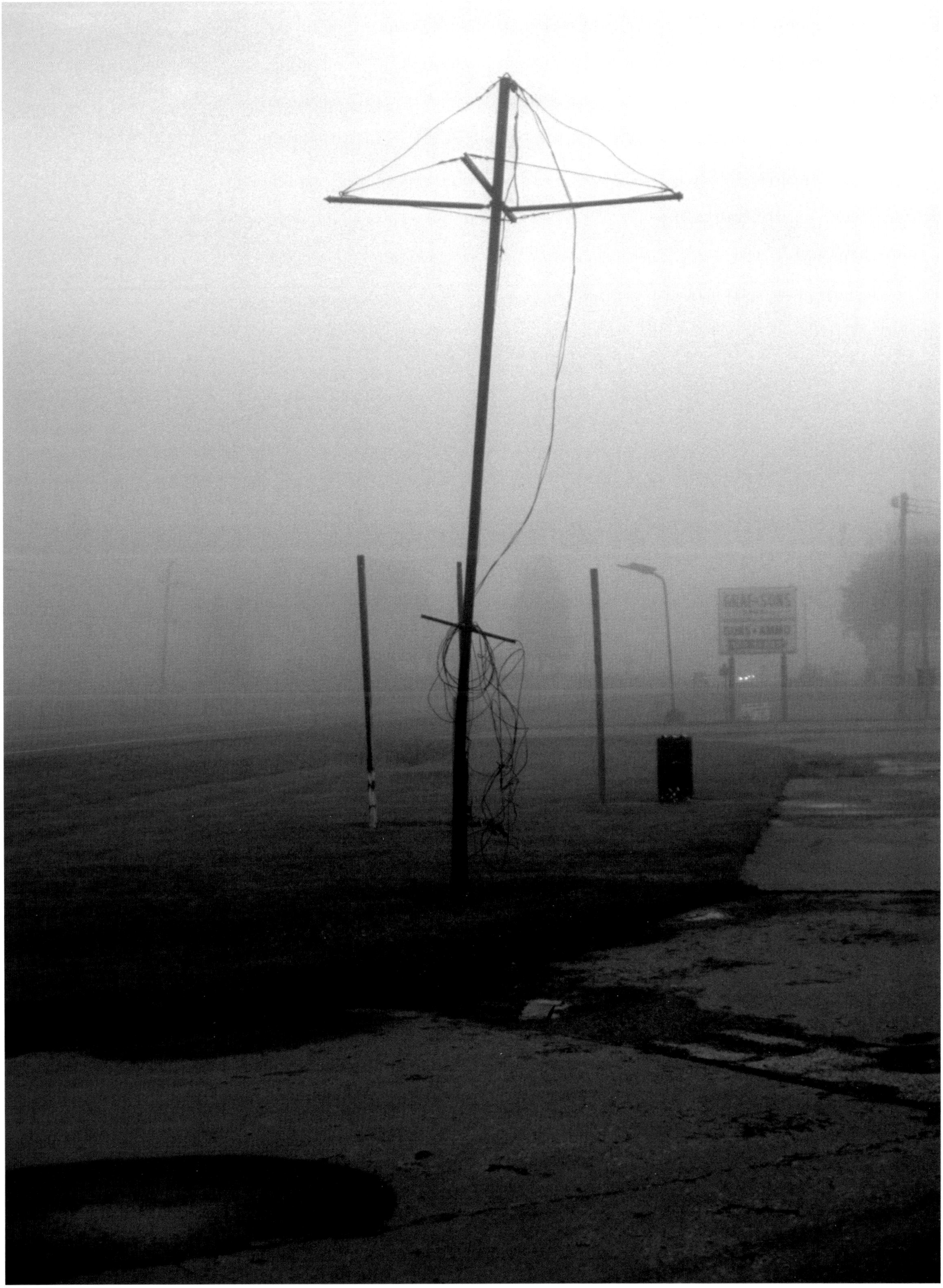

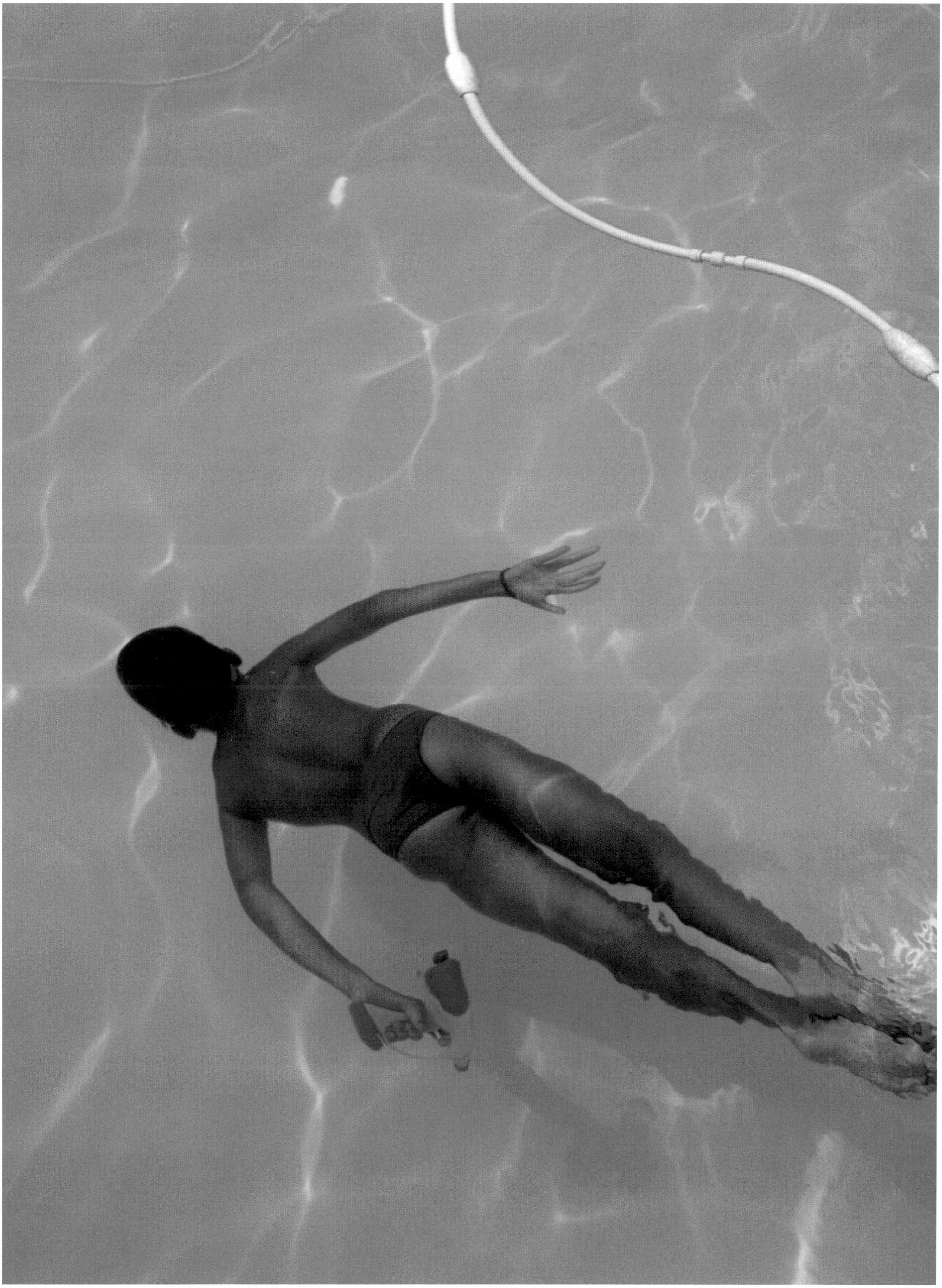

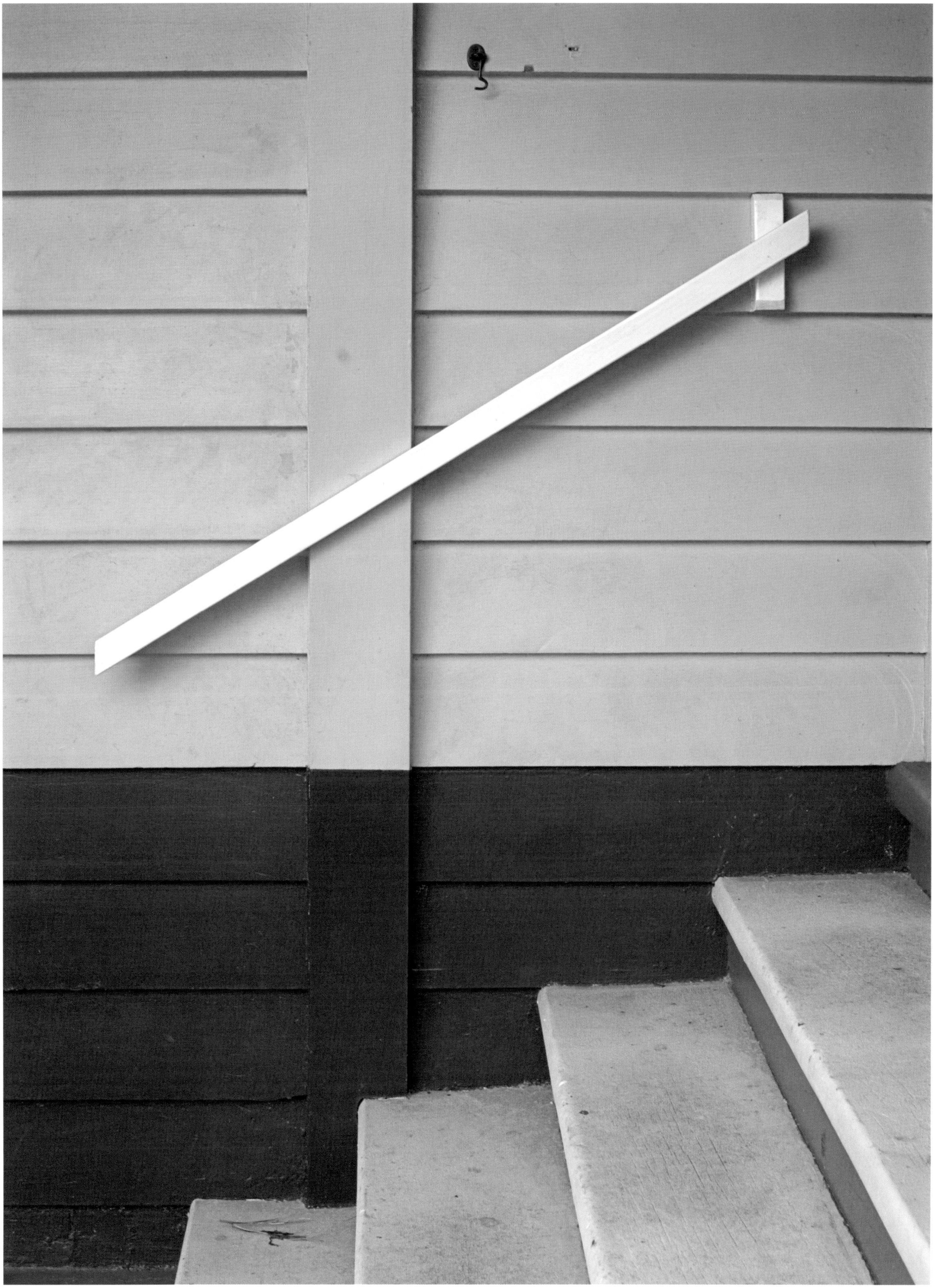

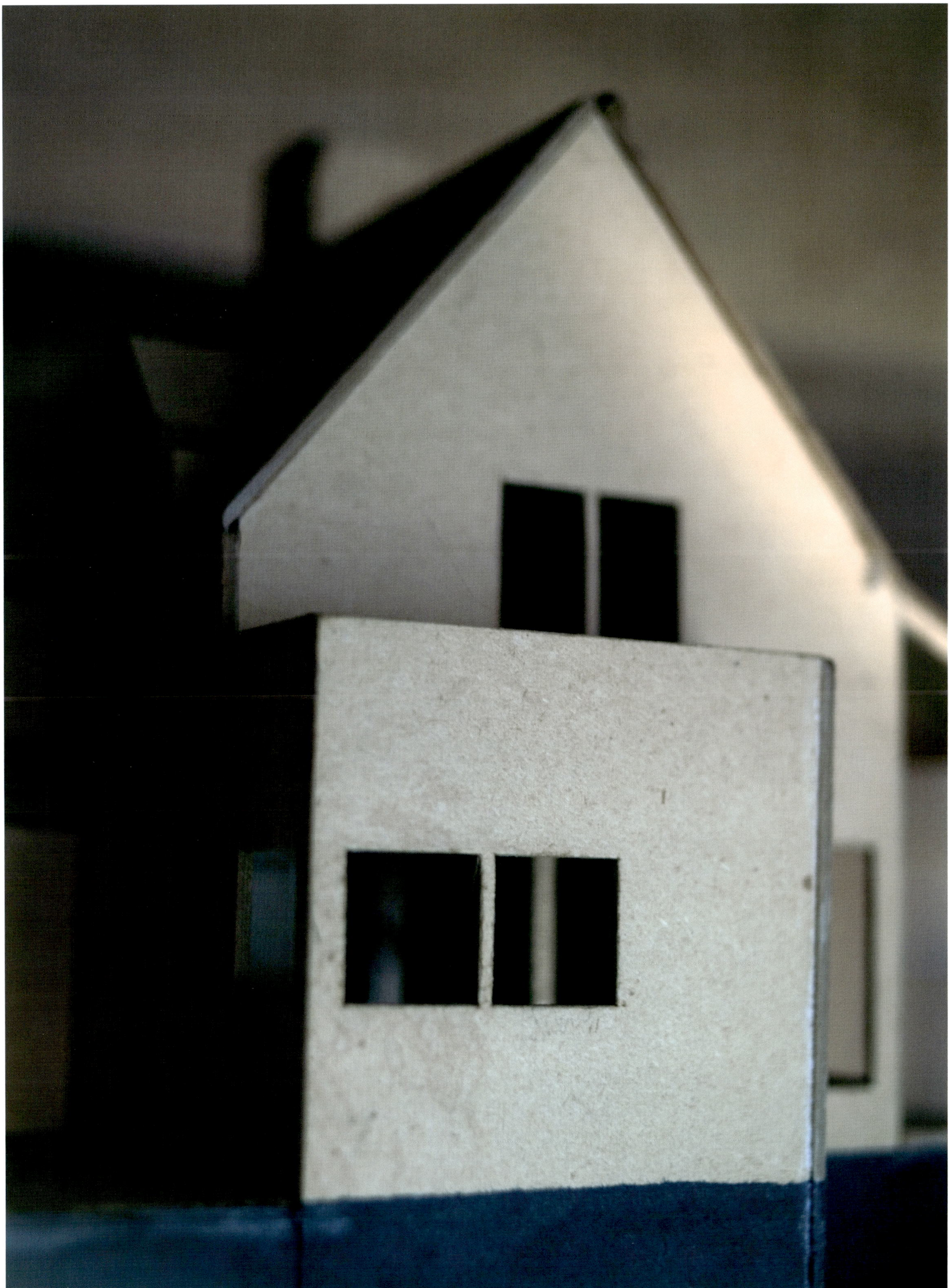

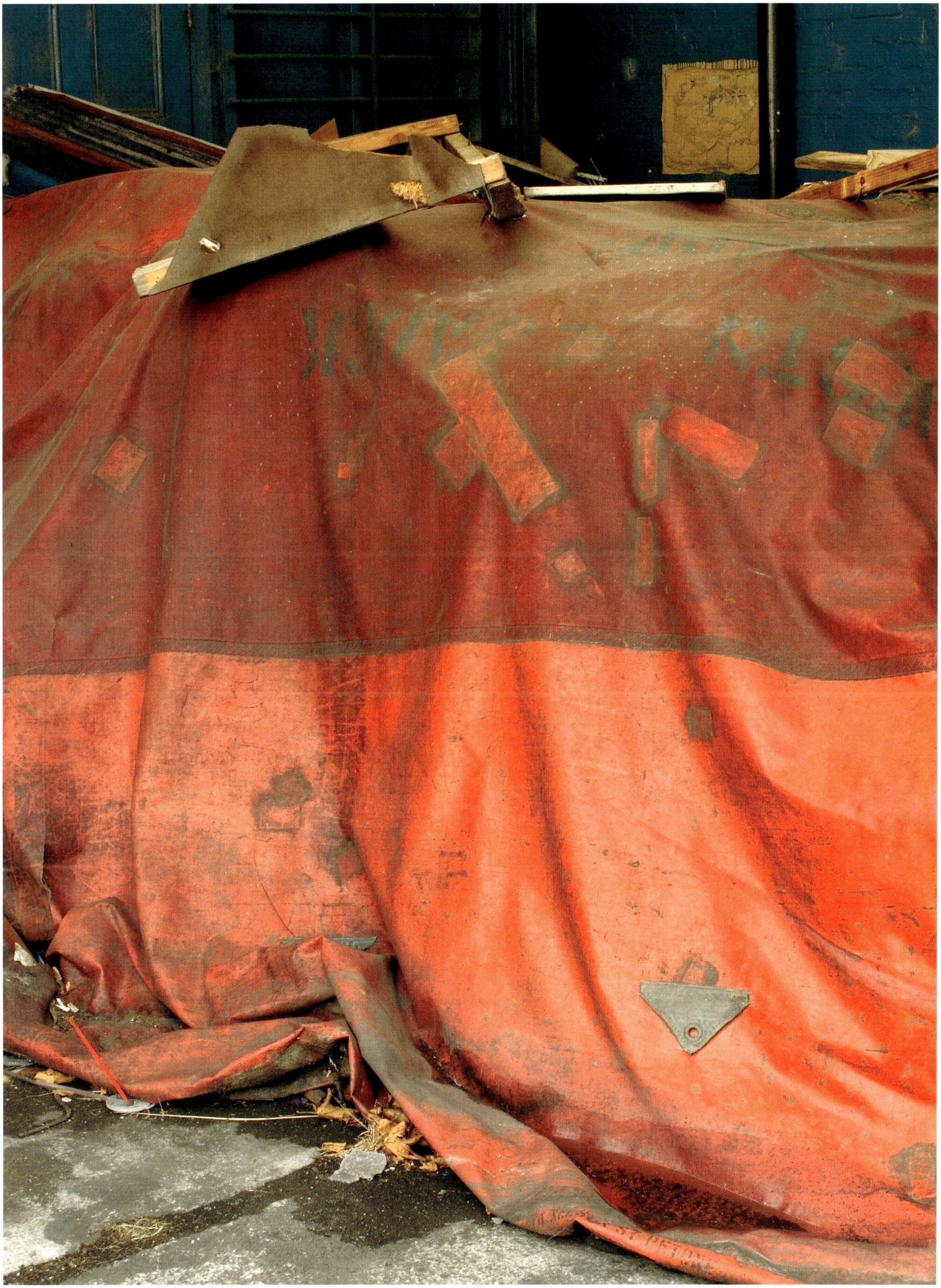

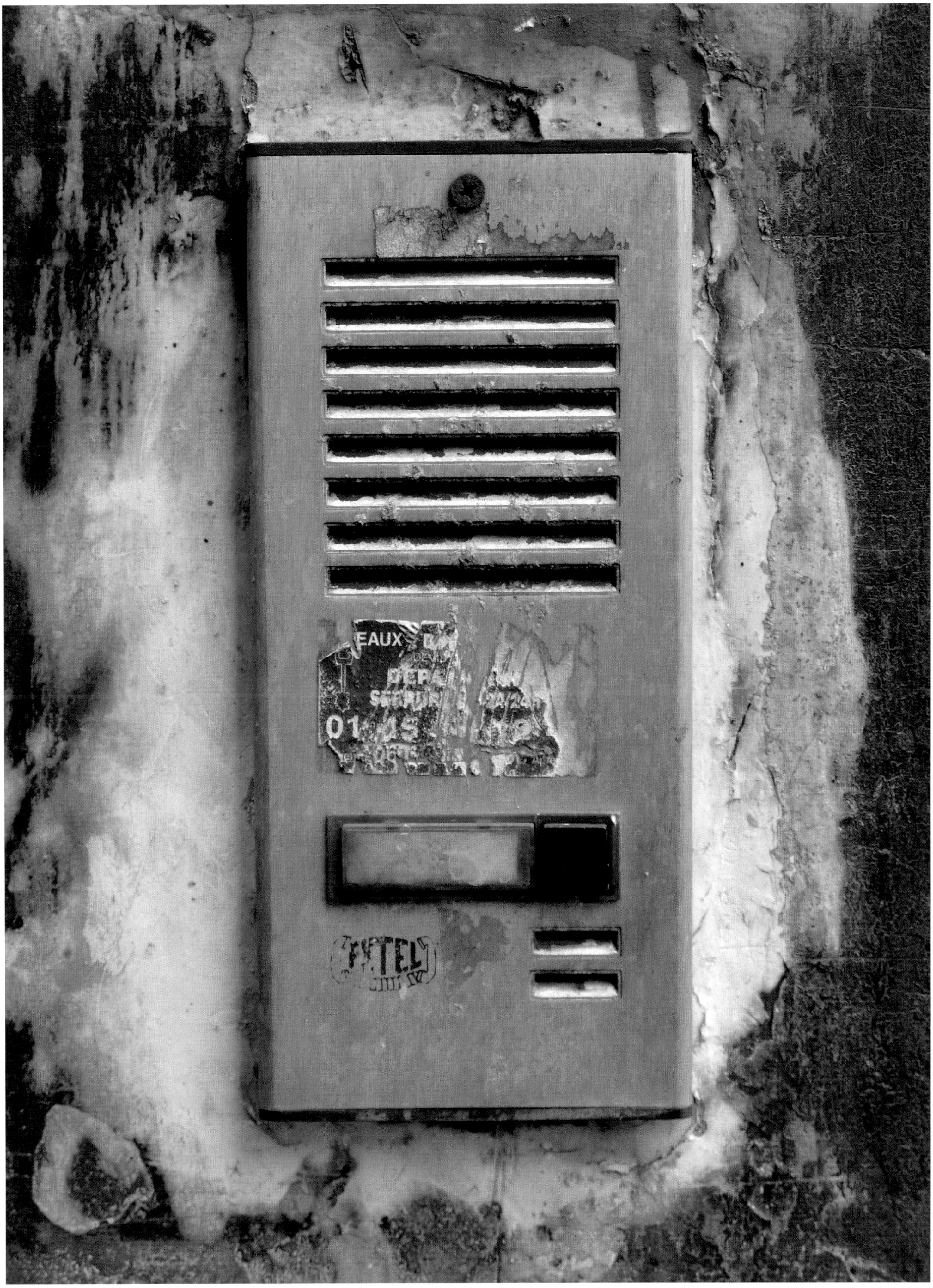
EAUX
01

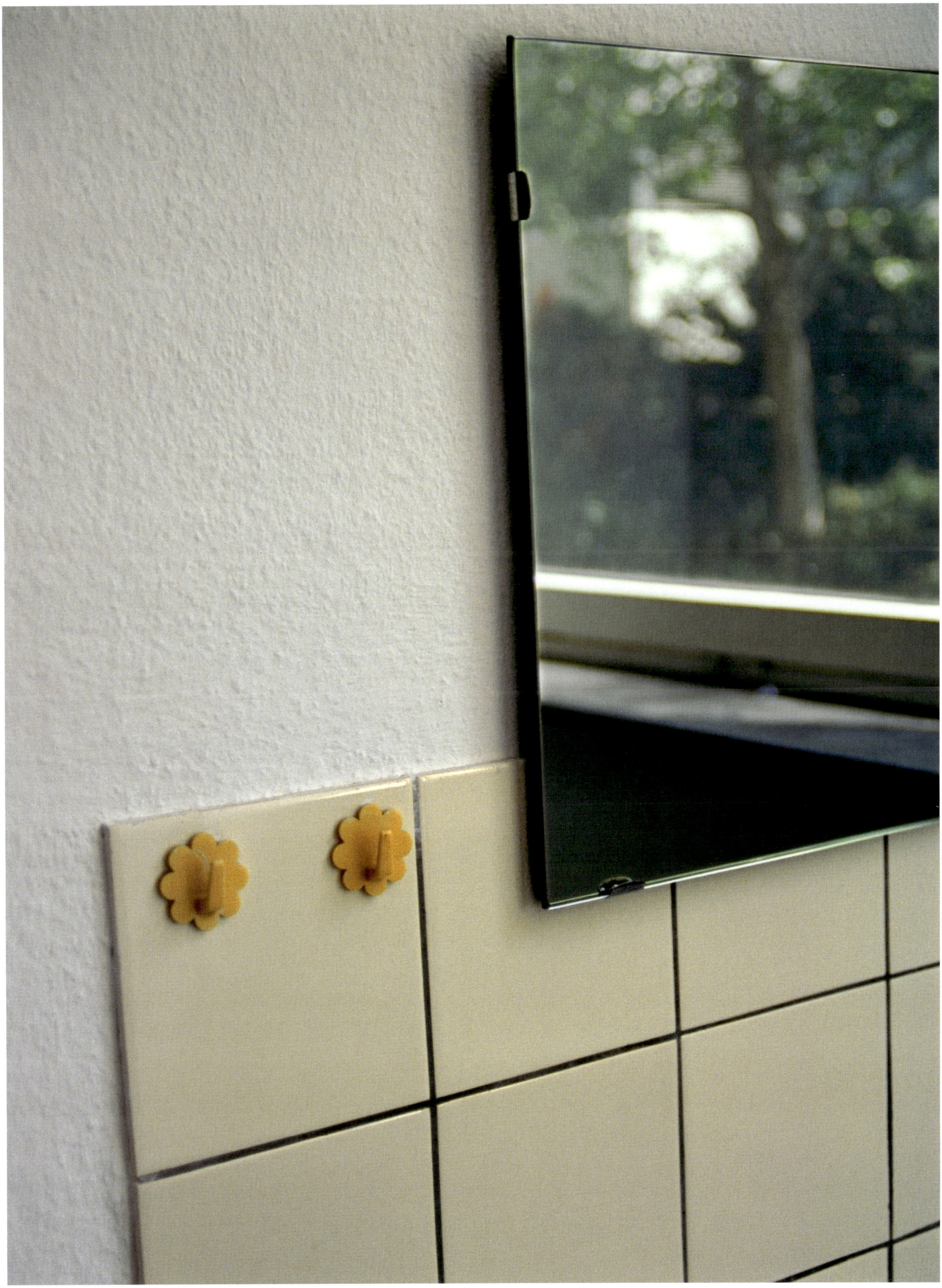

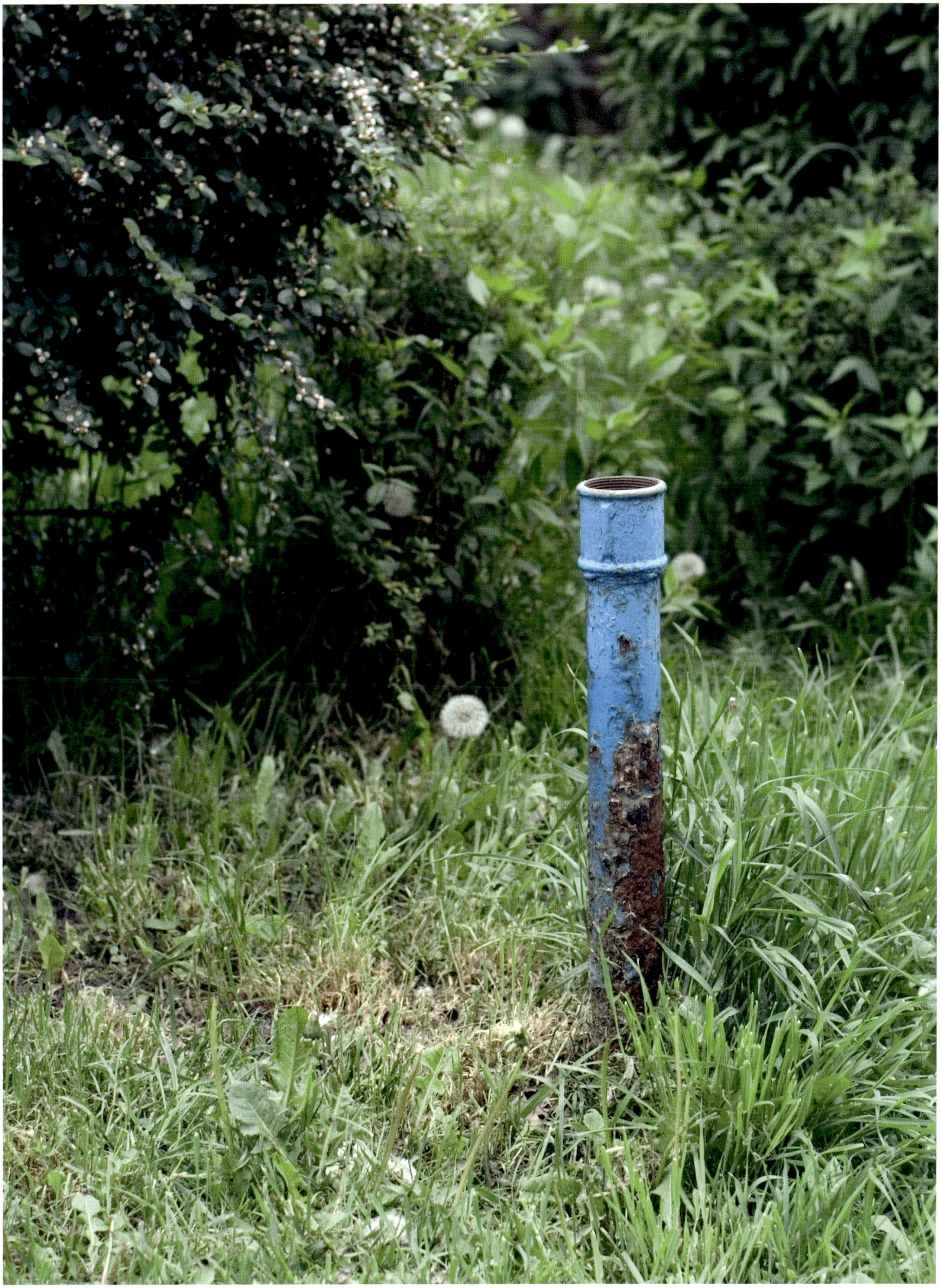

The images

Image processing
Kehrer Design (René Henoch, Jürgen Hofmann)

Design and production
Kehrer Design (Katharina Stumpf)

Frontispiece
Paris 2009

Cover images
Paris 2002 (front cover)
Paris 2002 (back cover)

Bibliographic information published by the Deutsche Nationalbibliothek
The Deutsche Nationalbibliothek lists this publication in the Deutsche Nationalbibliografie; detailed bibliographic data is available on the Internet at http://dnb.d-nb.de.

www.harveybenge.com
www.harveybenge.blogspot.com

printed in Germany

ISBN 978-3-86828-147-7
www.kehrerverlag.com